HORSE SAYINGS

wit & wisdom
straight from the horse's mouth

By Bradford G. Wheler

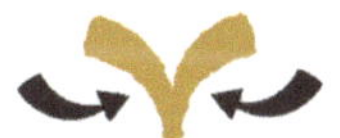

BookCollaborative.com
Cazenovia, NY 13035

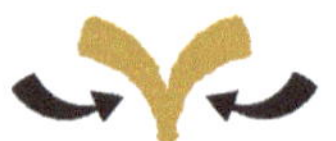

BookCollaborative.com
PO box 403
Cazenovia, NY 13035
BookCollaborative.com@gmail.com

ISBN-13 978-0-9822538-3-0

Library of Congress Control Number: 2011906601
Quotations, Horses, Art, Humor & Wit

PRINTER IN THE UNITED STATES OF AMERICA

Cover design by AuthorSupport.com
Interior design by Adina Cucicov, Flamingo Designs

Table of Contents

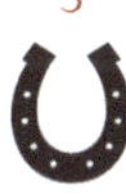

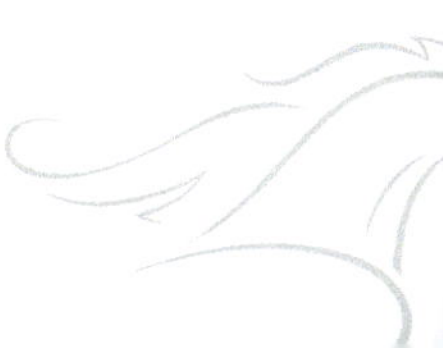

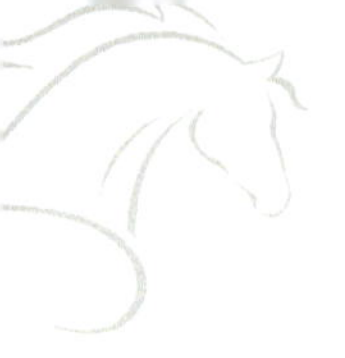

Introduction

I would like to thank everyone who participated in this project. In particular, I wanted to thank the artists and photographers who contributed their original works to this book.

It was exciting to check my email and find a wonderful range of new submissions from a wide variety of artists and photographers. The book features over 50 artists from 11 different countries. Many of the artists in this book are full time professional artists or photographers. Others love painting and photographing as a hobby. They exhibit a wonderful range of artistic styles. All are horse lovers.

I was very pleased to see how many of these artists are currently involved in animal rescue projects, giving generously of both their time and talent.

I established BookCollaborative.com to publish books based on the content provided by artists. The goal is to create a collaborative community to promote art in general. At the same time, artists have the opportunity to promote their own artwork in books. I also want it to be interesting and fun. I invite everyone to join us at www.BookCollaborative.com.

In selecting images for HORSE SAYINGS, I tried to be inclusive. However, some artwork simply didn't fit the theme of this book. Other artwork did not make the cut due to various factors, such as missing the deadline, low image resolution, etc.

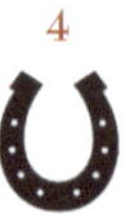

Printing color books with Lightening Source Inc.'s on demand system is about six times as expensive as printing black and white books. This factor limits the page count of a reasonably priced color book. It's my hope that as technology progresses, the price for color on demand printing will come down. This would allow greater flexibility in the size of color books as well as the number of pages.

This book would not have been possibly without the help of many others. They include Adina Cucicov of Flamingo Design, who has done a beautiful job with the book's interior design, Nancy Kelner who turns my sloppy first drafts into a workable format, Tom Lyga of eMarketMyBiz.com who helped with all things web related, and Simon, Ethan, and others from the Apple store One to One training team who patiently keep teaching me. I would like to thank my lovely wife Julie for her support on this project and everything else.

I'm sure this book includes errors. For those I apologize.

Most of all I hope people enjoy *"HORSE SAYINGS; wit & wisdom straight from the horse's mouth."*

BRADFORD G. WHELER

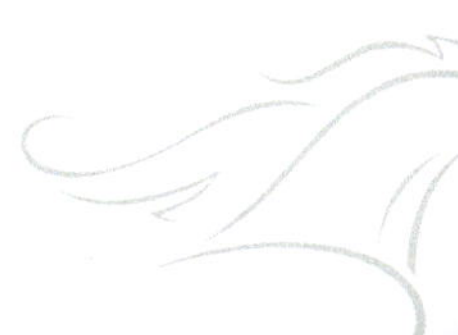

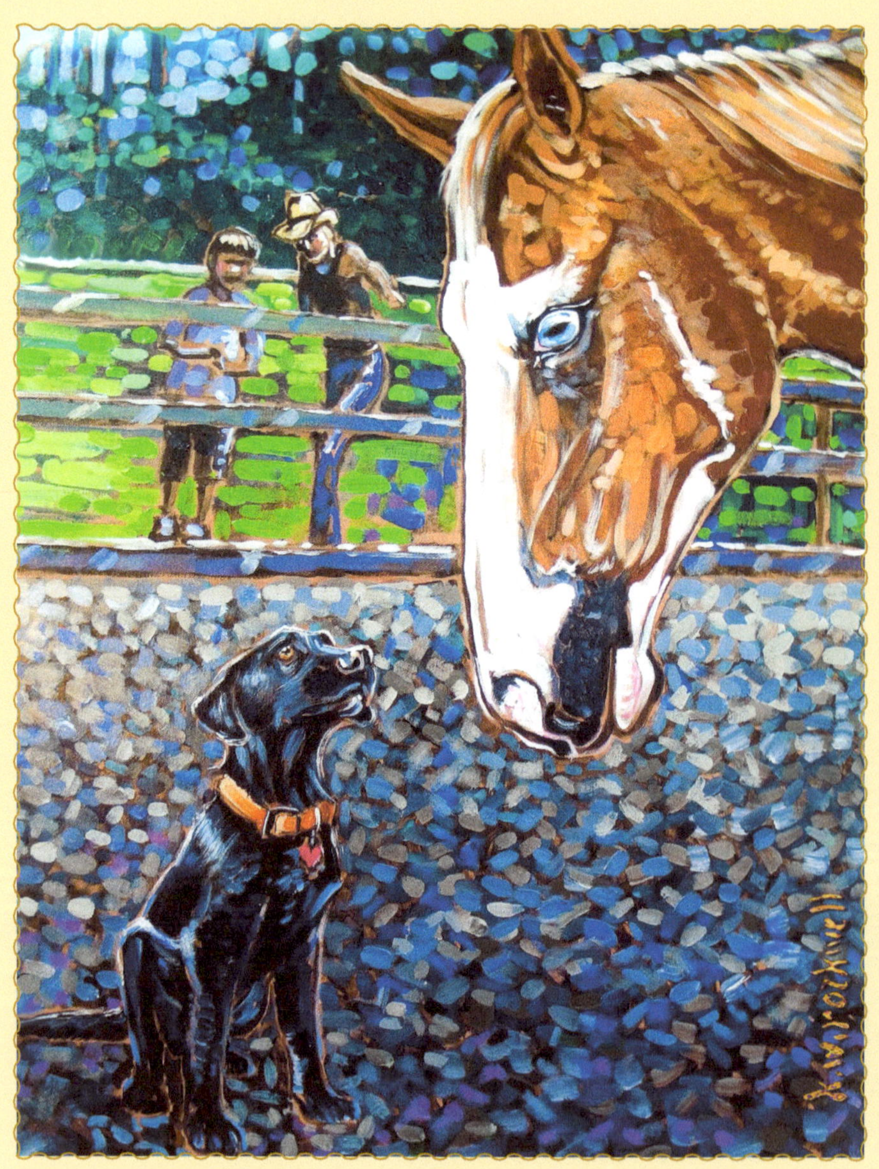

Kevin Rockwell

CHAPTER 1

The Bond

To many, the words love, hope, and dreams are synonymous with horses.

Oliver Wendell Holmes, Sr. (1809-1894)

My horses are my friends, not my slaves.

Reiner Klimke, (1936-1999)

Far back, far back in our dark soul the horse prances.

D. H. Lawrence, (1885-1930)

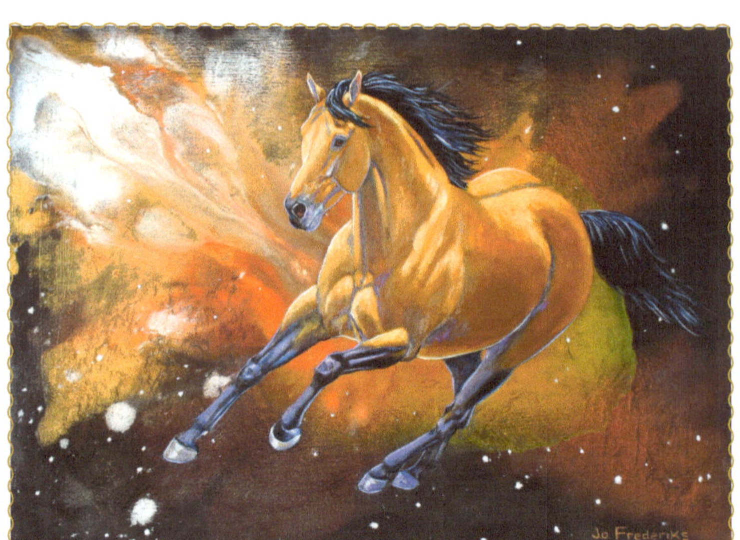

Jo Frederiks

There is a touch of divinity even in brutes, and a special halo about a horse that should forever exempt him from indignities.

Herman Melville, (1819-1891)

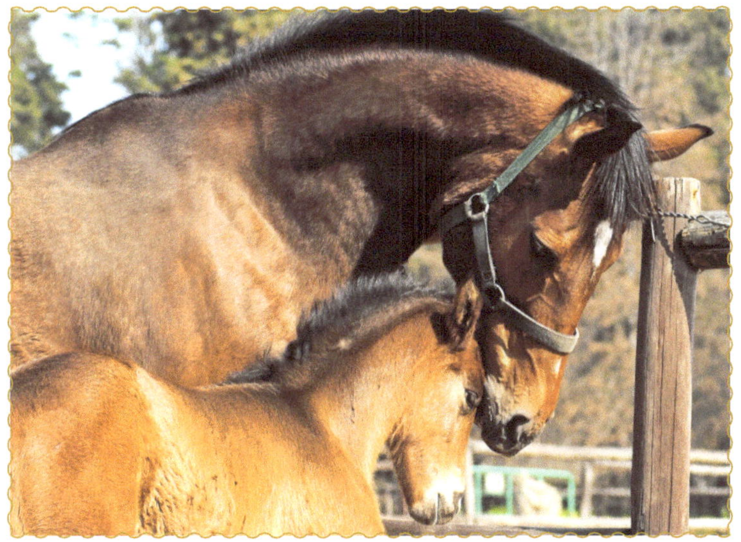

Leigh Willson

A good man will take care of his horses and dogs, not only while they are young, but also when they are old and past service.

Plutarch, (46-120)

He doth nothing but talk of his horse.

William Shakespeare, (1564-1616)

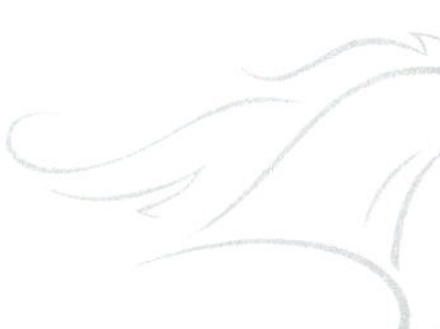

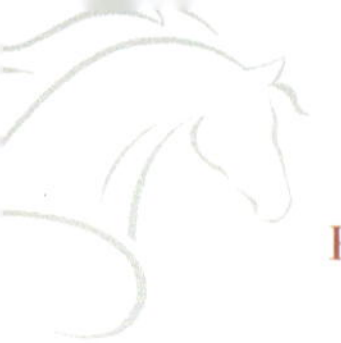

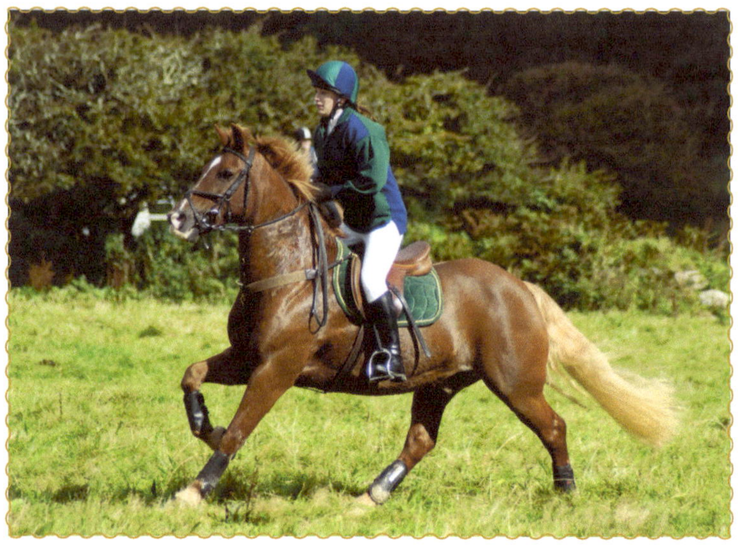

Hannah Tippett

Young men have often been ruined through owning horses, or through backing horses, but never through riding them, unless of course they break their necks, which, taken at a gallop, is a very good death to die.

Sir Winston Churchill, (1874-1965)

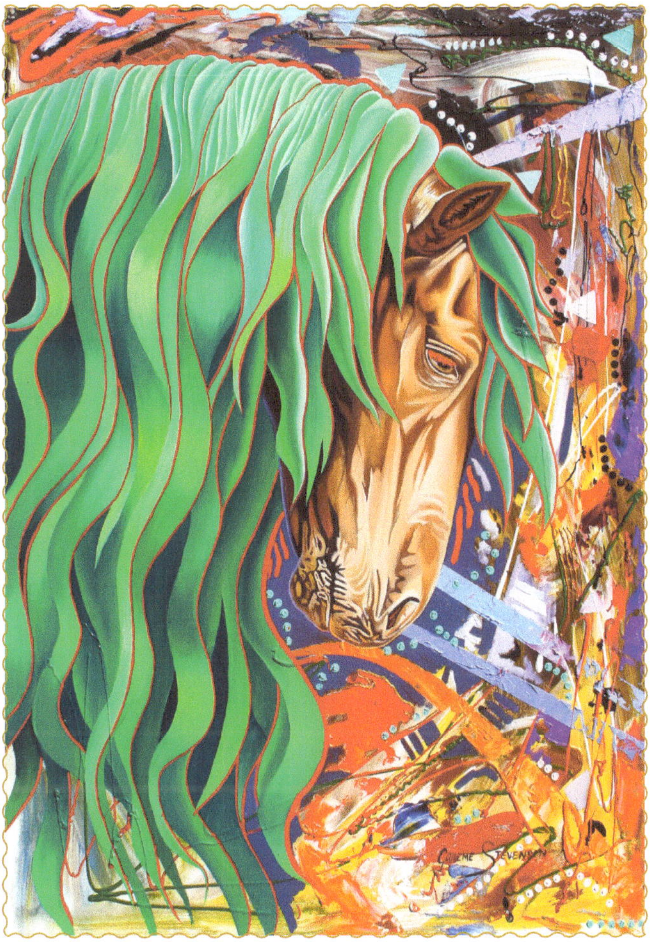

Graeme Stevenson

Honor lies in the mane of a horse.

Herman Melville, (1819-1891)

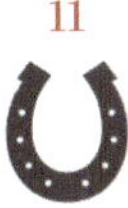

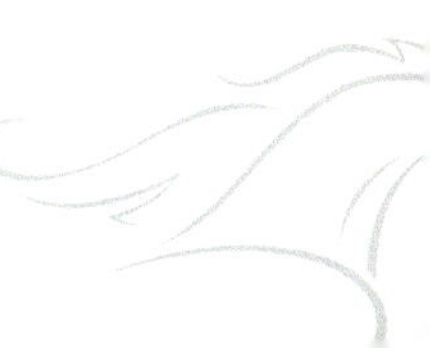

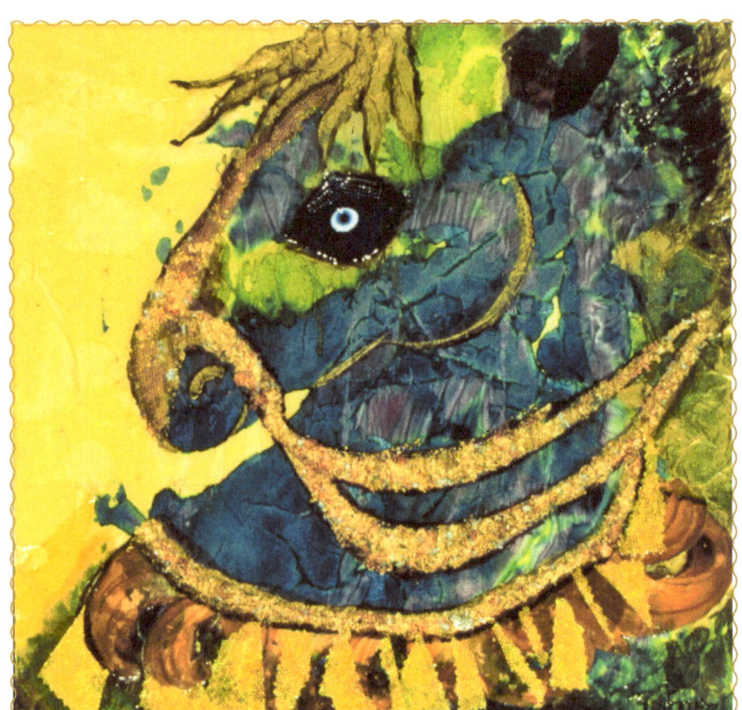

Ione Citrin

A Chieftain was challenged to a duel by an enemy and killed, and when his adversary came to strip his body of his armor, his horse kicked him and bit him till he died.

Pliny The Elder, (23-79)

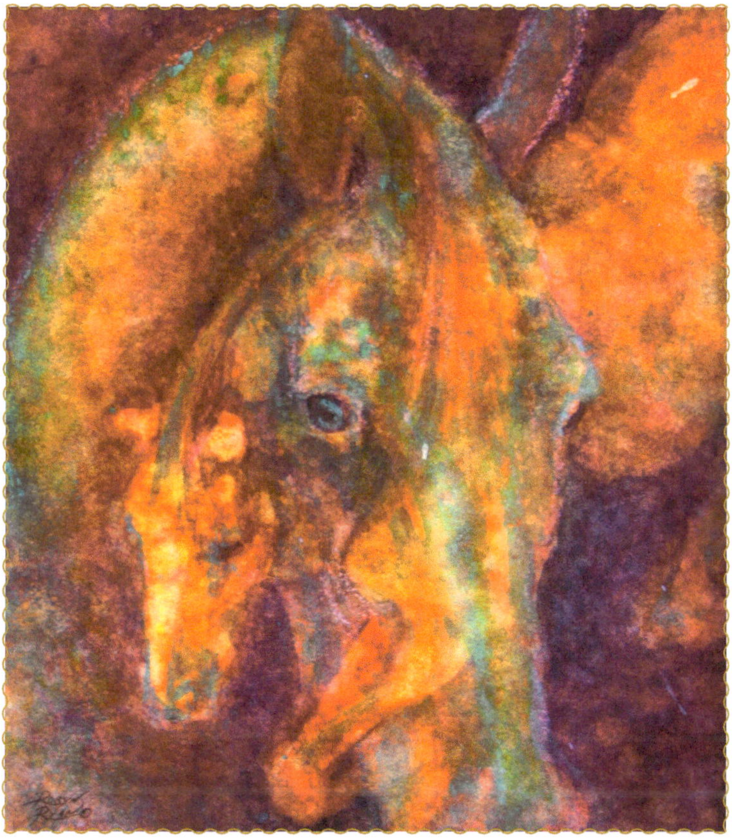

Robyn Ryan

Another horse, when his blinkers were removed and it found out that the mare he had covered was his dam, made for a precipice and committed suicide.

Pliny The Elder, (23-79)

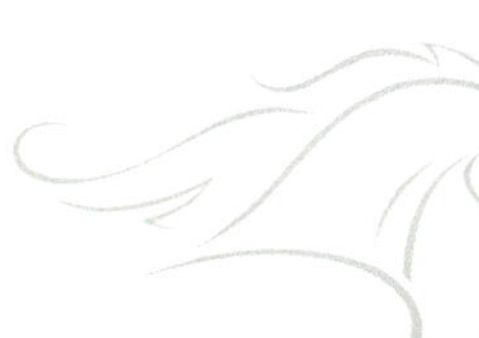

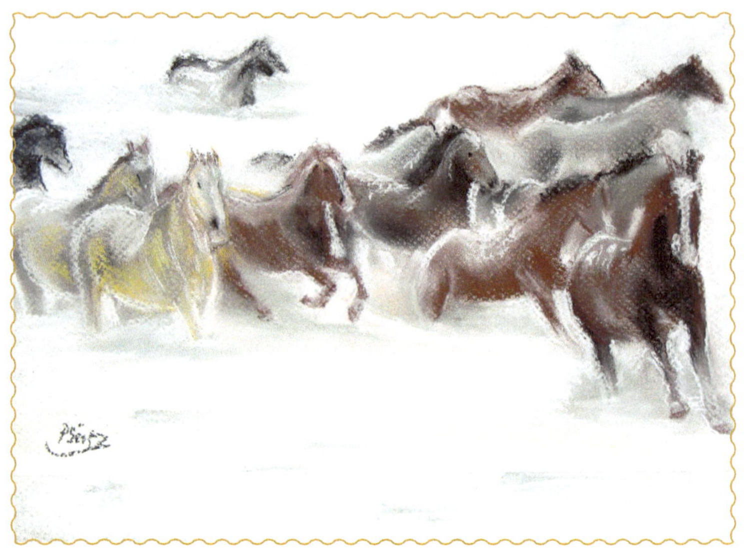

Patricia Seitz

Wherever man has left his footprint in the long ascent from barbarism to civilization, we will find the hoof print of a horse beside it.

John Trotwood Moore, (1874-1965)

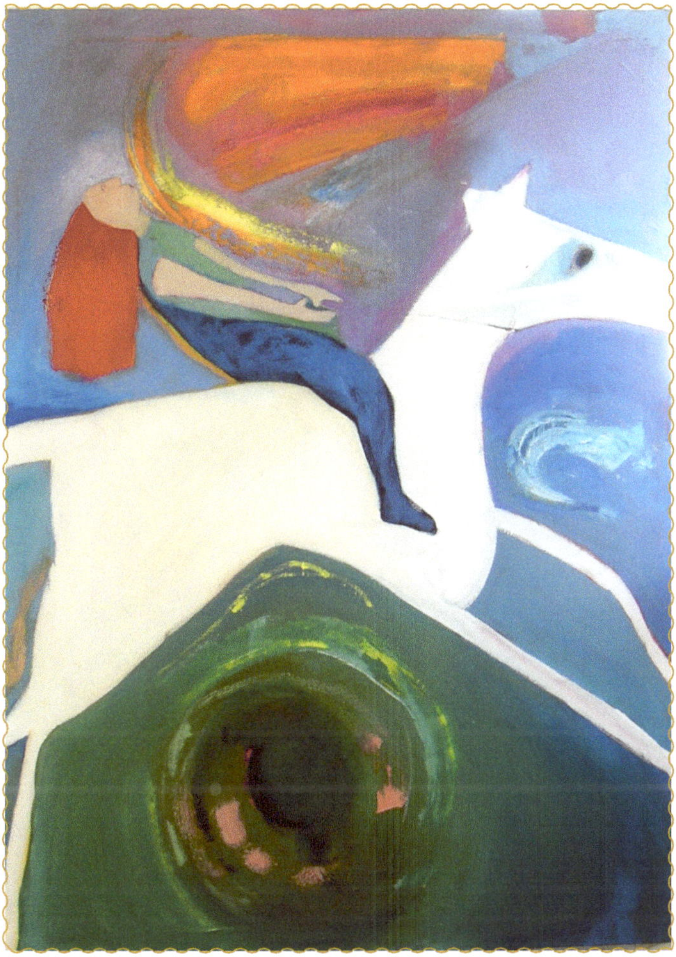

Carolyn Schlam

A canter is a cure for every evil.

Benjamin Disraeli, (1804-1881)

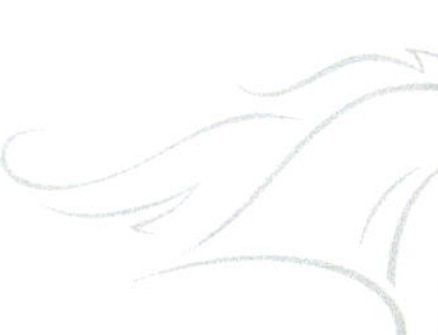

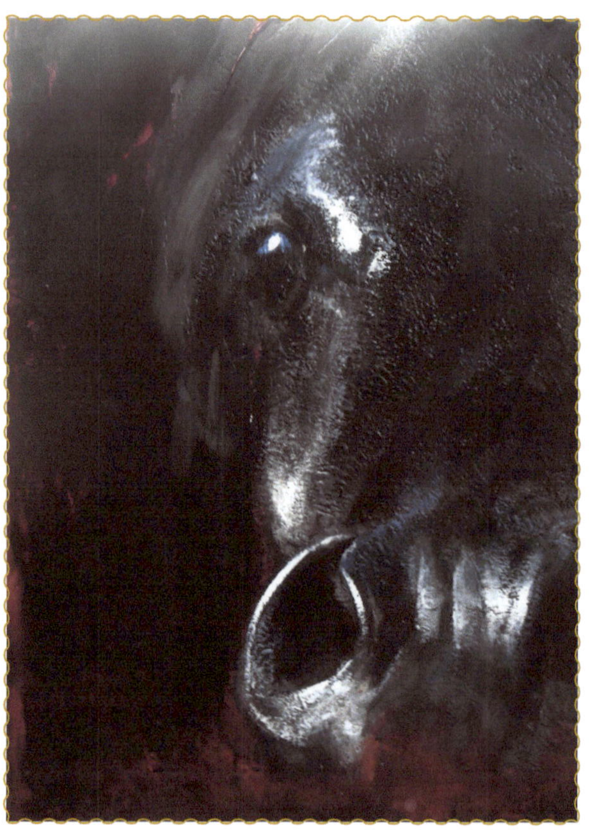

Rick Young

Here lies the body of my good horse, The General. For years he bore me around the circuit of my practice and all that time he never made a blunder. Would that his master could say the same.

John Tyler's epitaph for his horse, (1790-1862)

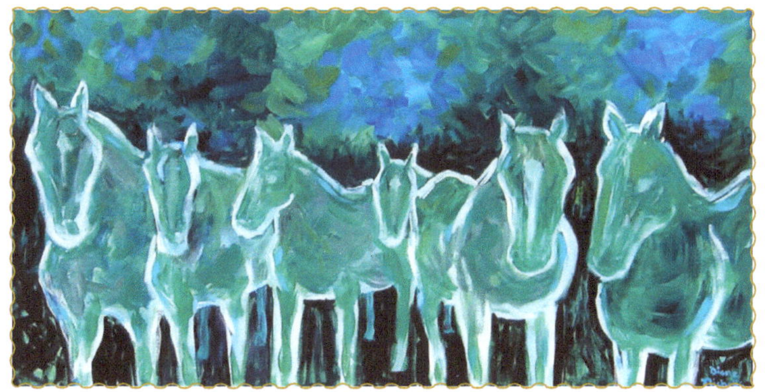

Diane Nicholls

In grateful and reverent memory of the Empire's horses (some 375,000) who fell in the Great War (1914 – 1918). Most obediently, and often most painfully, they died.

Memorial at Church of St. Jude, London

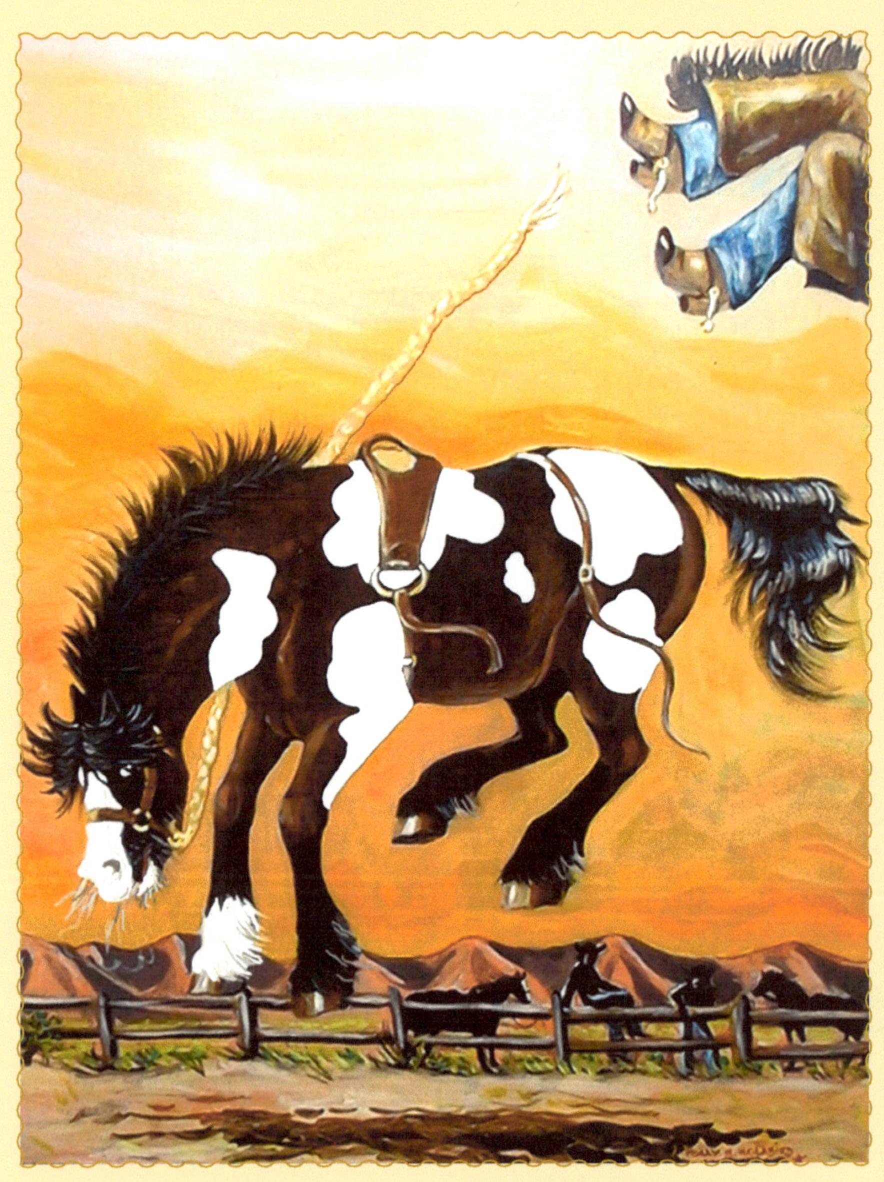

Polly Holabird

CHAPTER 2

Humor

Tell me why a hearse horse snickers hauling a lawyer's bones.

Carl Sandberg, (1876-1967)

Ascot is so exclusive that it is the only racecourse in the world where the horses own the people.

Art Buchwald, (1925-2007)

I'd horsewhip you . . . if I had a horse.

Groucho Marx, (1890-1977)

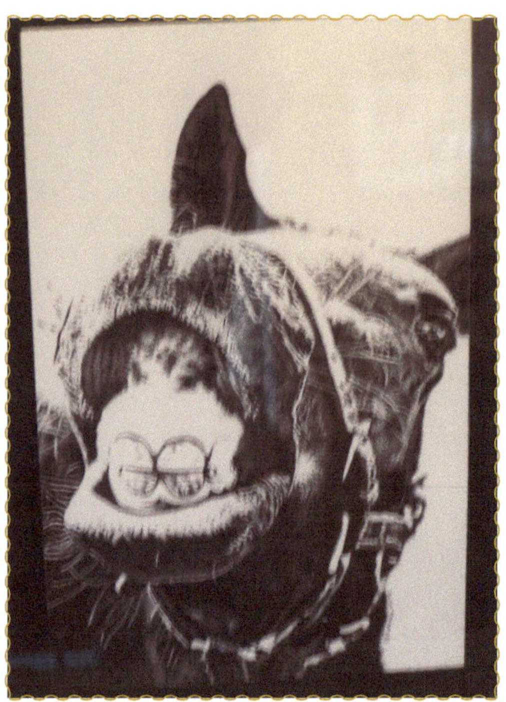

Gilda Meyers

A mule will labor ten years willingly and patiently for you, for the privilege of kicking you once.

William Faulkner, (1897-1962)

They say he rides as if he's part of the horse, but they don't say which part.

Robert Sherwood, (1896-1955)

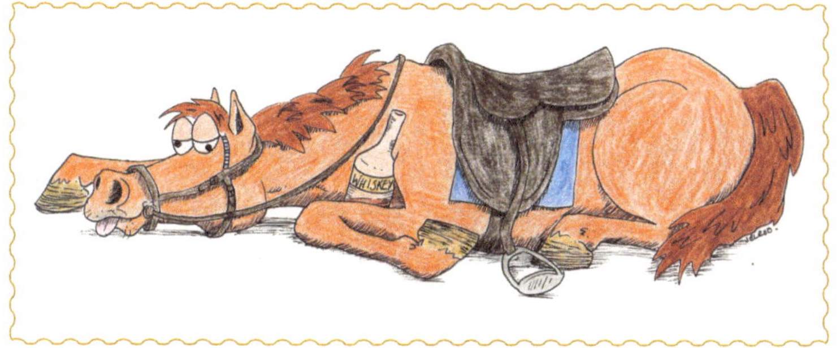

Joanne Elrod

It takes a good deal of physical courage to ride a horse. This, however, I have. I get it at about forty cents a flask, and take it as required.

Stephen Leacock, (1869-1944)

The daughter who won't lift a finger in the house is the same child who cycles madly off in the pouring rain to spend all morning mucking out a stable.

Sarah Armstrong, (b. 1968)

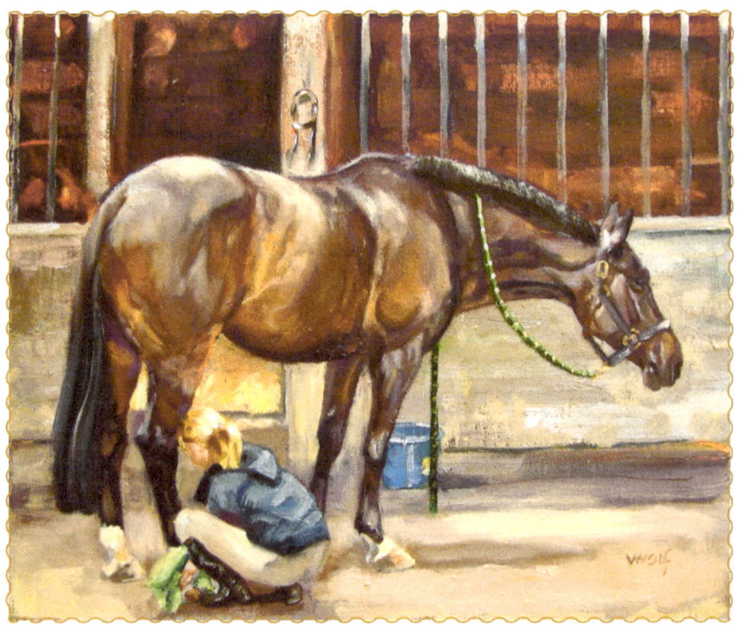

Valarie Wolf

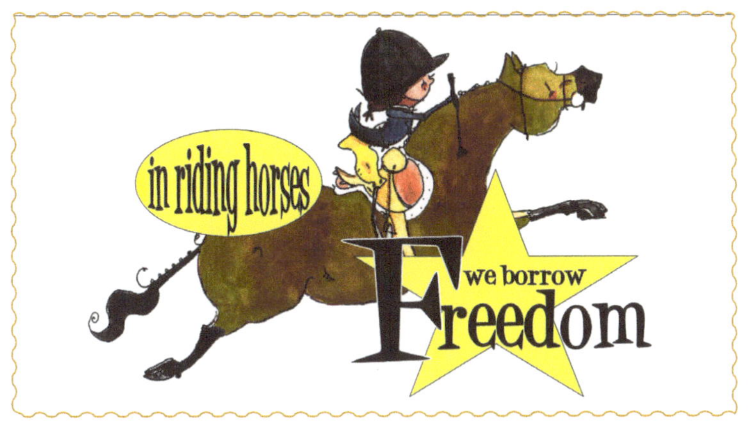

Dana Bauer

A horse is dangerous at both ends and uncomfortable in the middle.

Ian Fleming, (1908-1964)

You can lead a horse to water, but if you can teach him to roll over and float on his back, then you got something.

Joe E. Lewis, (1902-1971)

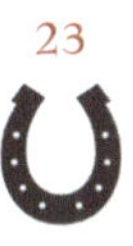

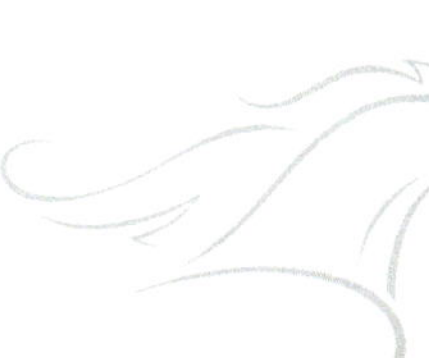

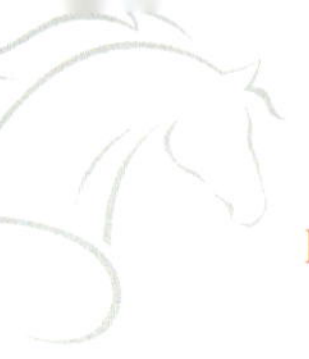

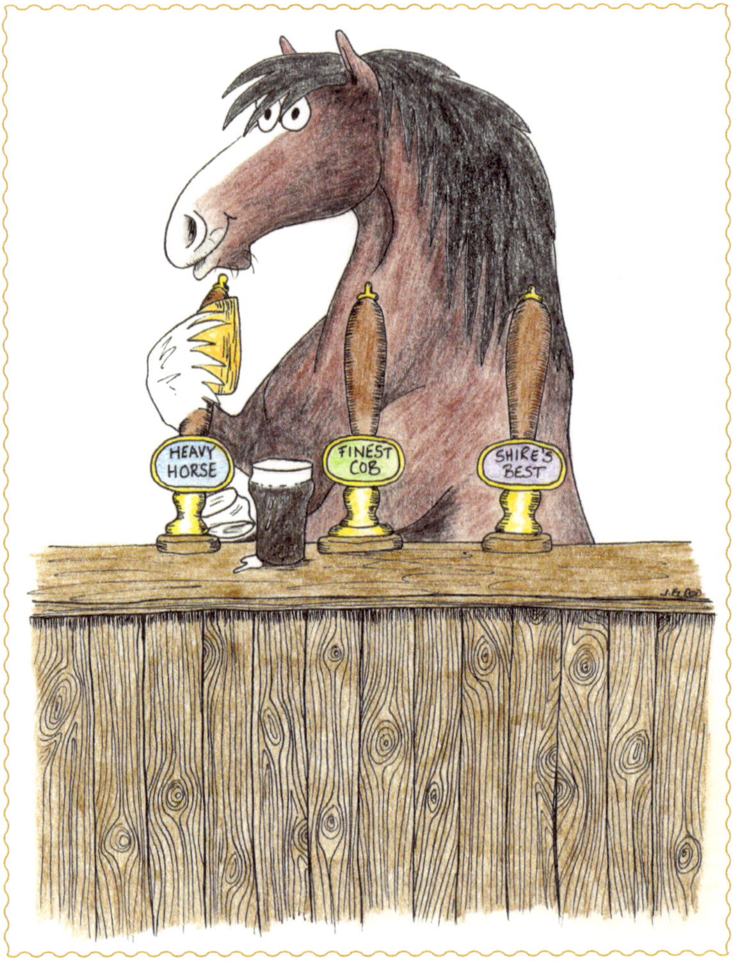

Draft Horse, Joanne Elrod

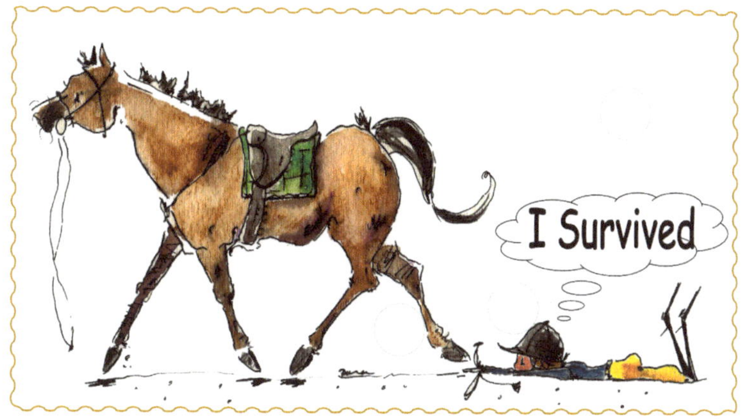

Dana Bauer

I ride horses because it's the only sport where I can exercise while sitting down.

Joan Hansen, (b. 1958)

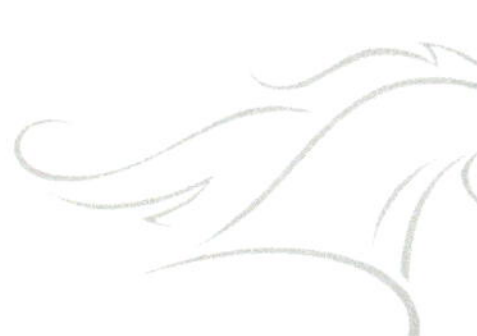

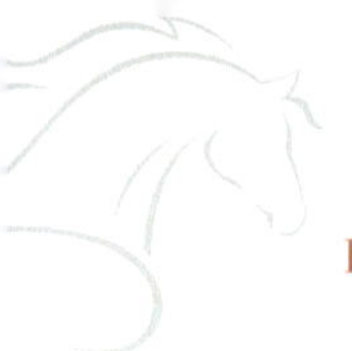

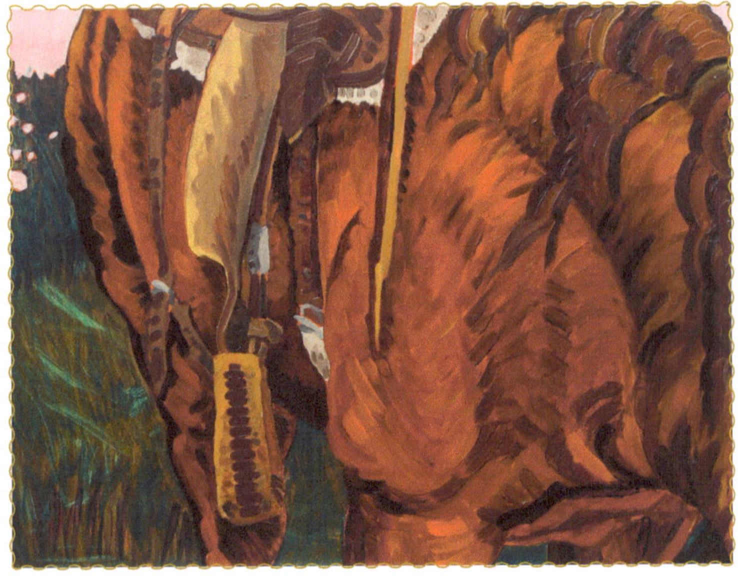

Erica Veit

MUSTANG, n. An indocile horse of the western plains. In English society, the American wife of an English nobleman.

Ambrose Bierce, (1842-1914)

The one thing I do not want to be called is First Lady. It sounds like a saddle horse.

Jacqueline Kennedy Onassis, (1929-1994)

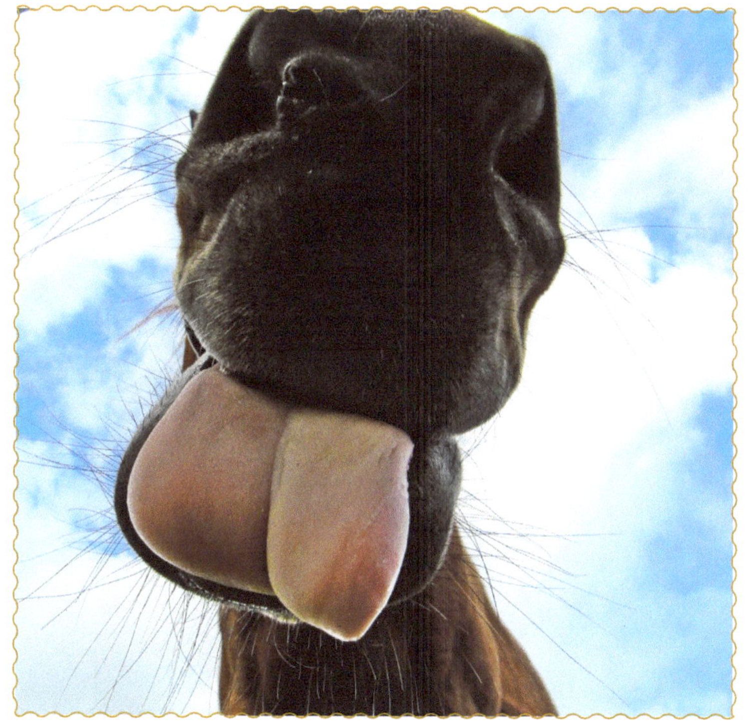

Pamela Utton

In Westerns you were permitted to kiss your horse but never your girl.

Gary Cooper, (1901-1961)

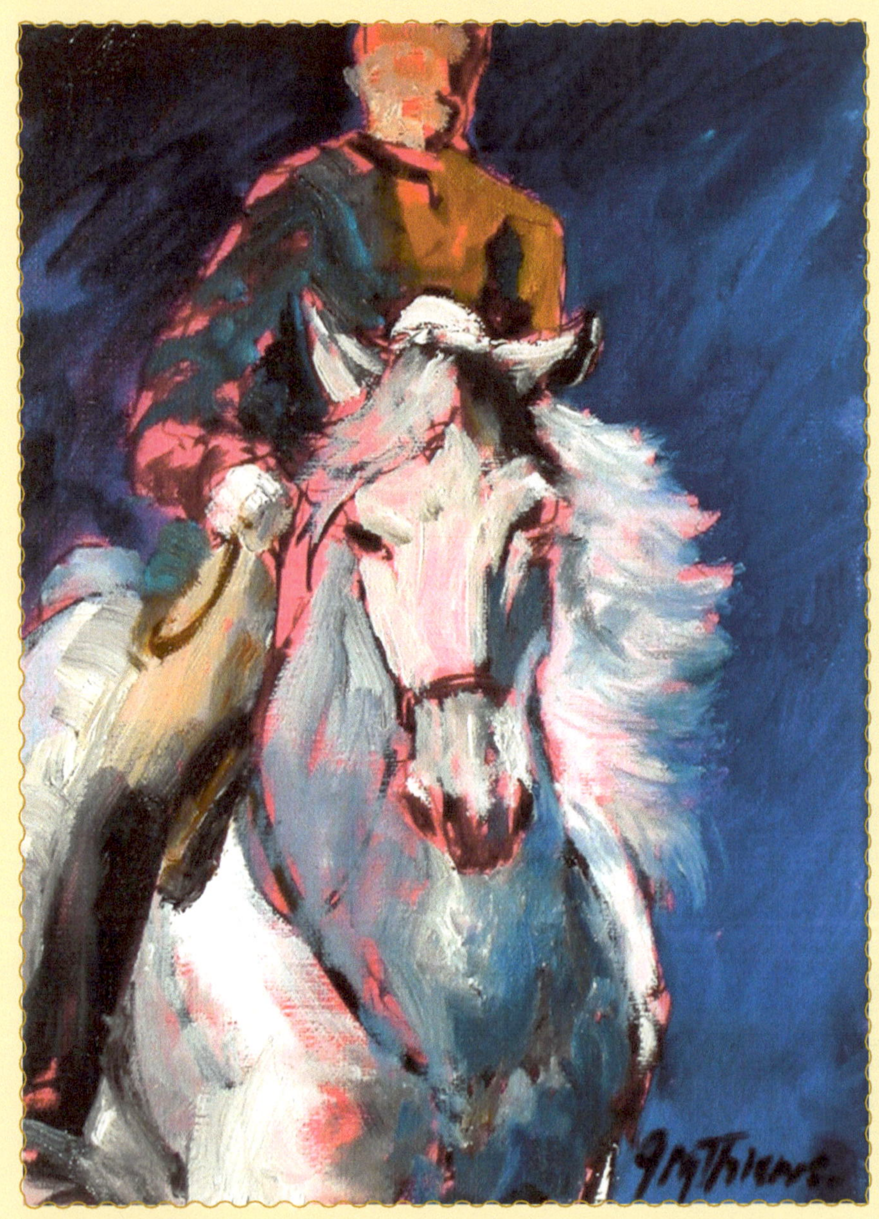

Jeanne M. Thieme

CHAPTER 3

The Starting Gate

The race is not always to the swift nor the battle to the strong—but that's the way to bet.

Damon Runyan, (1880-1946)

It is not best that we all think alike, it is difference of opinion that makes horse races.

Mark Twain, (1835-1910)

You're never a super horse until you're retired. Any horse can be beaten on any given day.

Angel Cordero, Jr., (b. 1942)

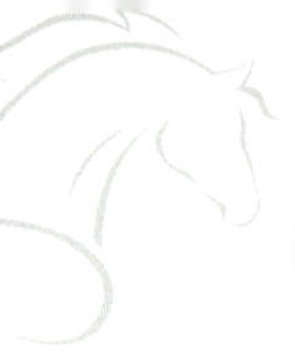

I am still under the impression there is nothing alive quite so beautiful as a thoroughbred horse.

John Galsworthy, (1867-1933)

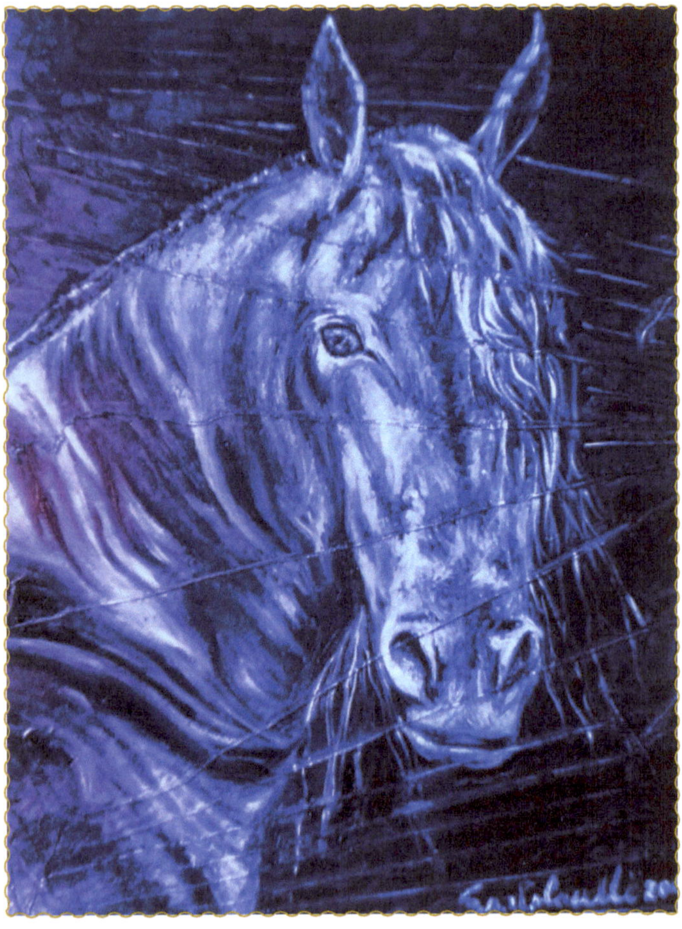

Segio Bartolacelli

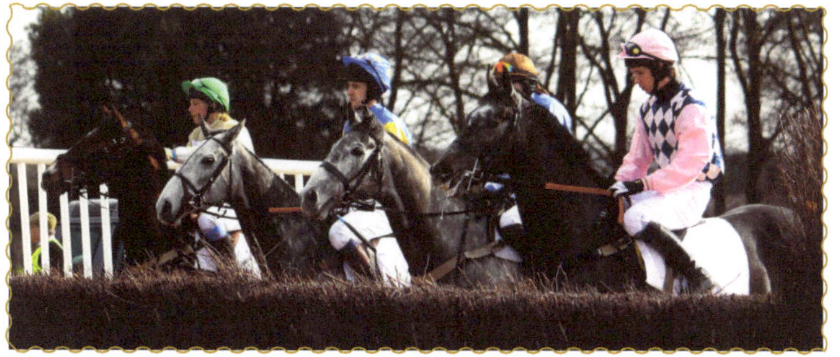

Kerry Ball

You know horses are smarter than people. You never heard of a horse going broke betting on people.

Will Rogers, (1879-1935)

I hope I break even. I need the money.

Joe E. Lewis, (1902-1971)

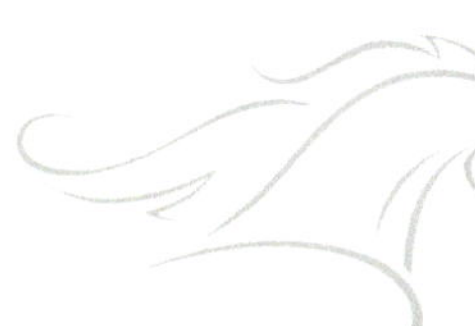

There's no sense in whipping a tired horse, because he'll quit on you. More horses are whipped out of the money than into it.

Eddie Arcaro, (1916-1997)

A horse gallops with his lungs, perseveres with his heart, and wins with his character.

Federice Tesio, (1869-1954)

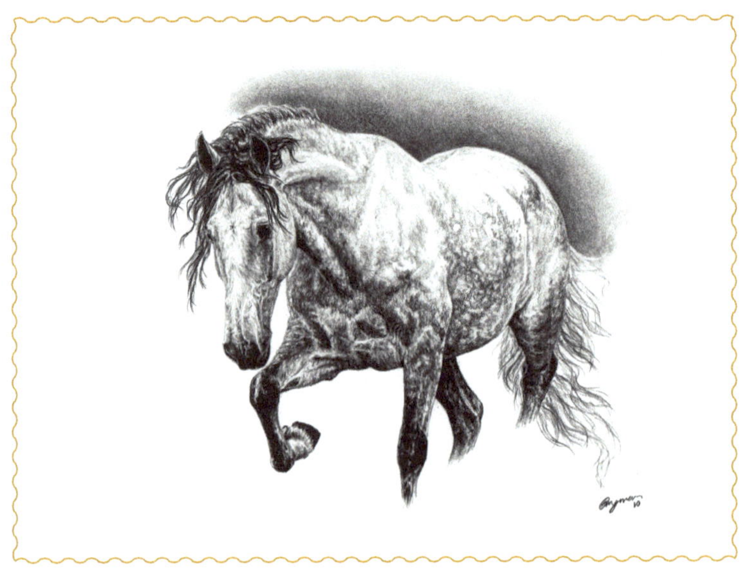

Emily Mayman

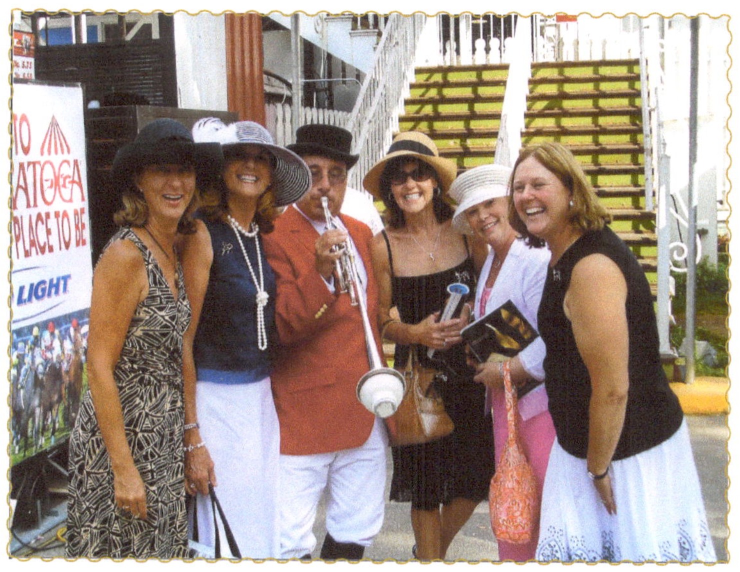

Julie Wheler

You're better off betting on a horse than betting on a man. A horse may not be able to hold you tight, but he doesn't wanna wander from the stable at night.

Betty Grable, (1916-1973)

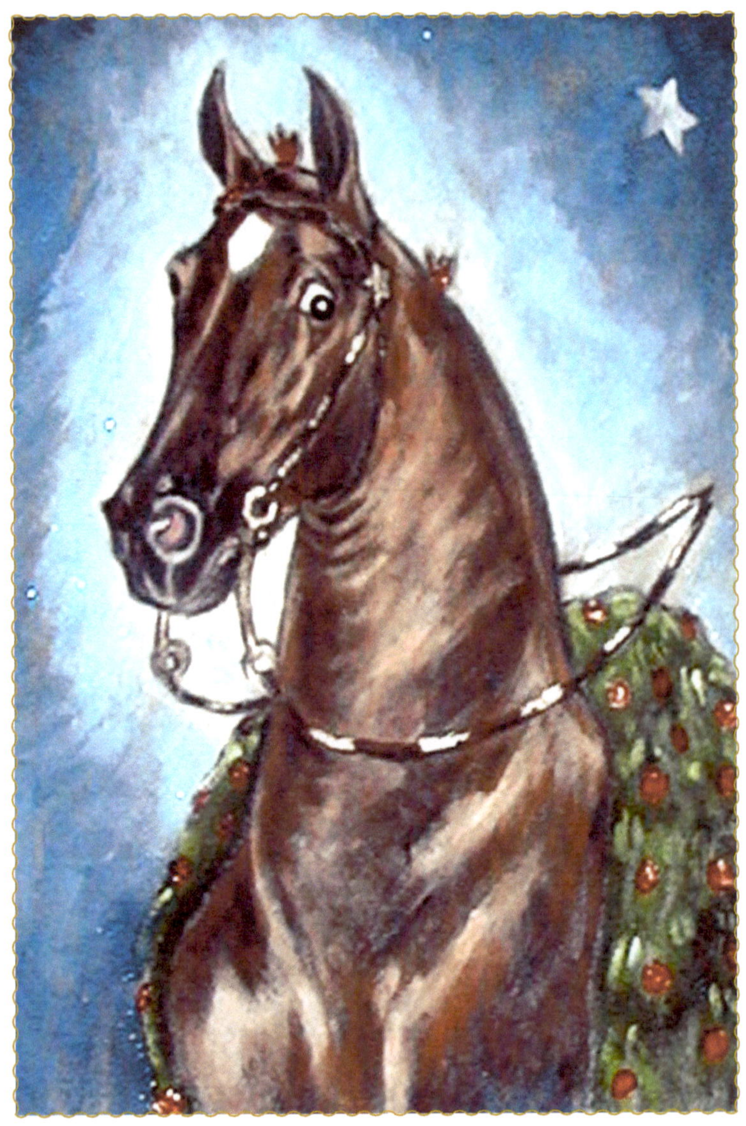

Polly Holabird

I played a great horse yesterday! It took seven horses to beat him.

The horse I bet on was so slow, the jockey kept a diary of the trip.

My horse's jockey was hitting the horse. The horse turns around and says "Why are you hitting me, there is nobody behind us!"

That was the first time I saw a horse start from a kneeling position.

My horse was so late getting home, he tiptoed into the stable.

I don't mind when my horse is left at the post. I don't mind when my horse comes up to me in the stands and asks "Which way do I go?" But when the horse I bet on is at the $2 window betting on another horse in the same race . . .

Henry Youngman, (1906-1998)

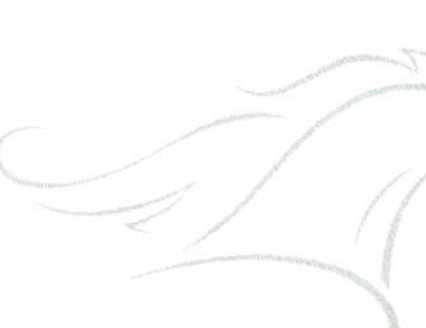

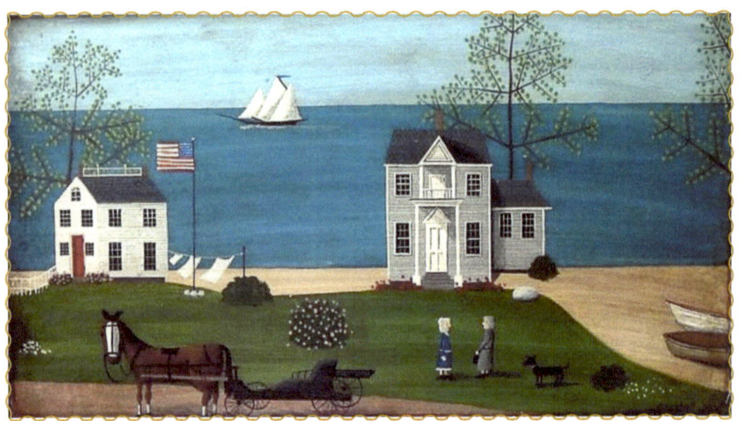

Tim Campbell

Horse sense is the good judgment that keeps horses from betting on people.

W.C. Fields (1880-1946)

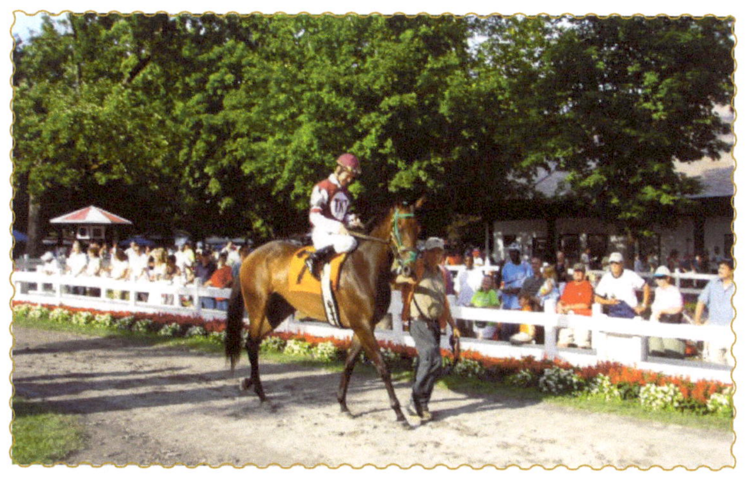

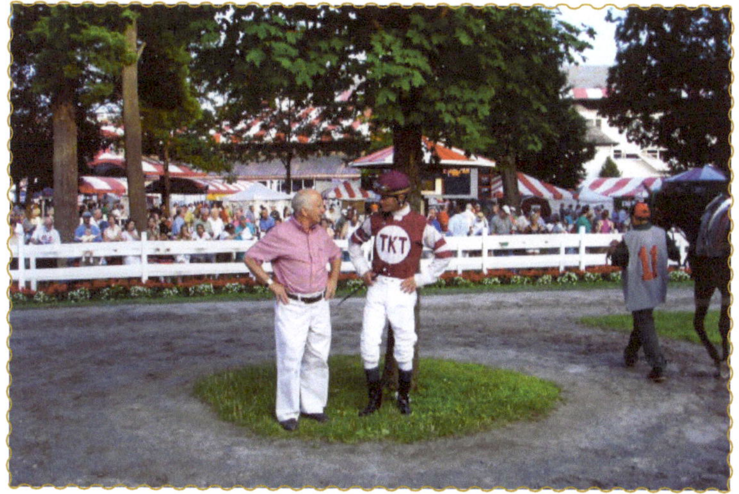

Julie Wheler

Jockey Calvin Borel on Money Oriented at Saratoga (top)
Trainer Culom O'Brien and Jockey Calvin Borel (Bottom)

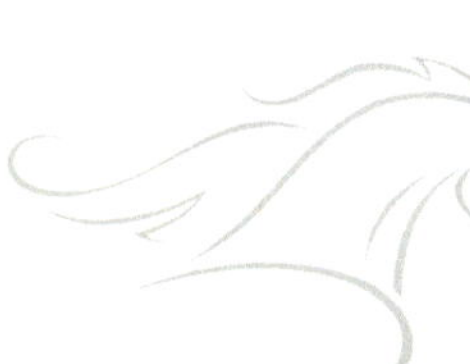

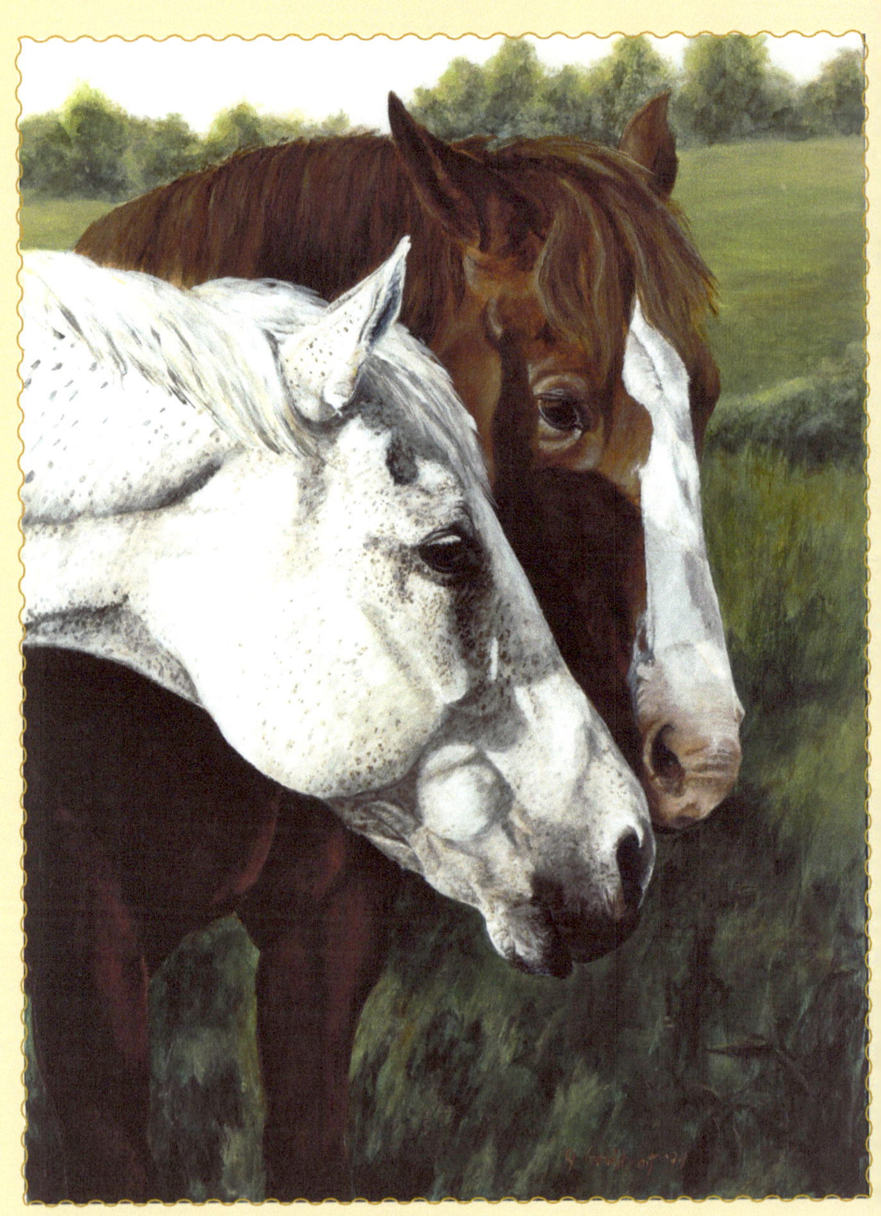

Judy Goldthwait

CHAPTER 4

Horse Sense

When you are on a great horse, you have the best seat you will ever have.

Sir Winston Churchill, (1874-1965)

All you need for happiness is a good gun, a good horse, and a good wife.

Daniel Boone, (1734-1820)

A good horse makes short miles.

George Eliot, (1819-1880)

Whoever said a horse was dumb, was dumb.

Will Rogers, (1879-1935)

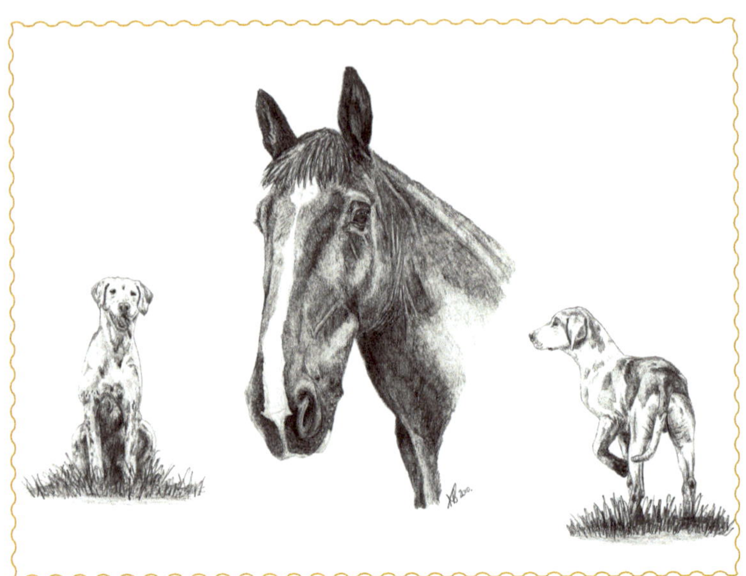

Faith Bailey

Some of my best leading men have been dogs and horses.

Elizabeth Taylor, (1932-2011)

No philosophers so thoroughly comprehend us as dogs and horses.

Herman Melville, (1819-1891)

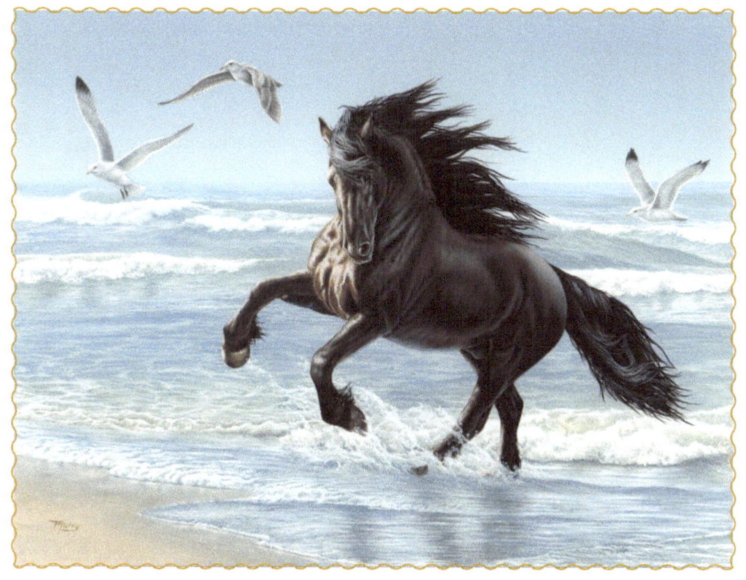

Dee Dee Murry

The horse, the horse: The symbol of surging potency and power of movement, of action, in man.

D. H. Lawrence, (1885-1930)

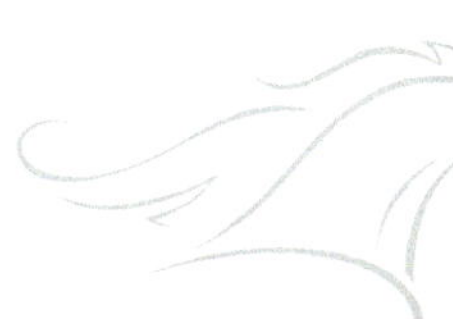

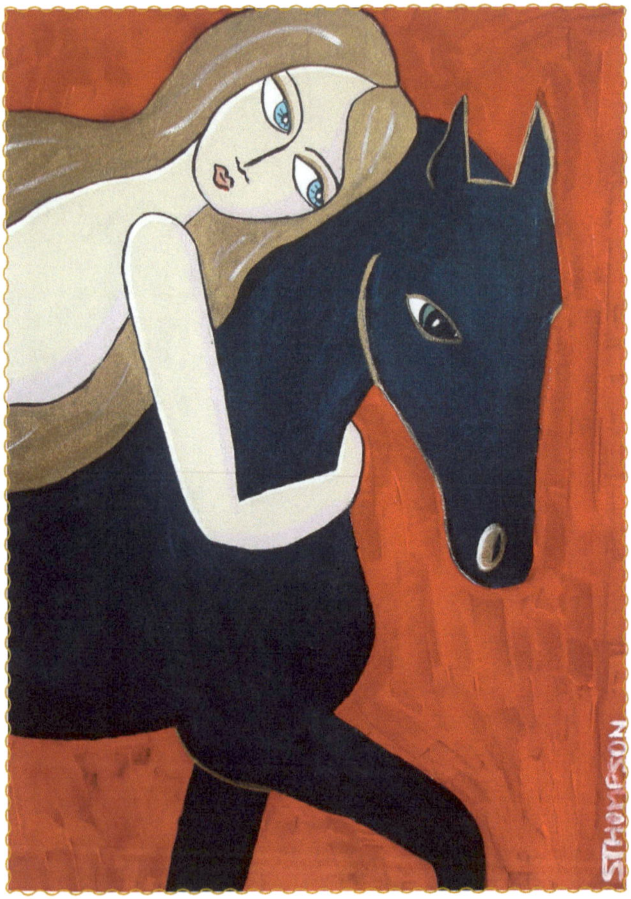

Samantha Thompson

Treat a horse like a woman and a woman like a horse. And they'll both win for you.

Elizabeth Arden, (1884-1966)

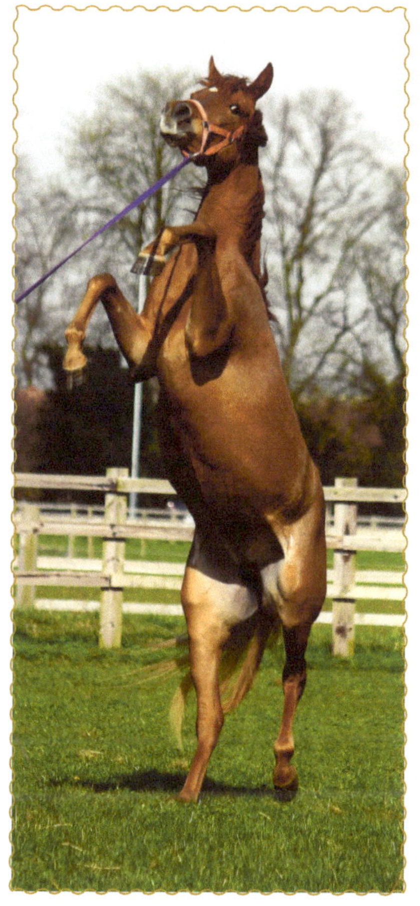

Kerry Ball

Few girls are as well shaped as a good horse.

Hannah Arendt, (1906-1975)

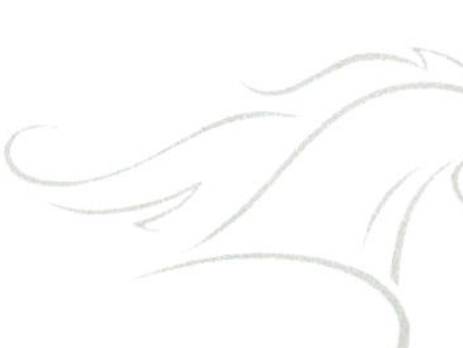

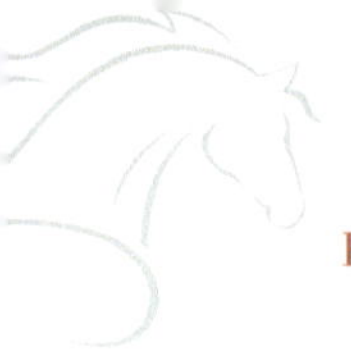

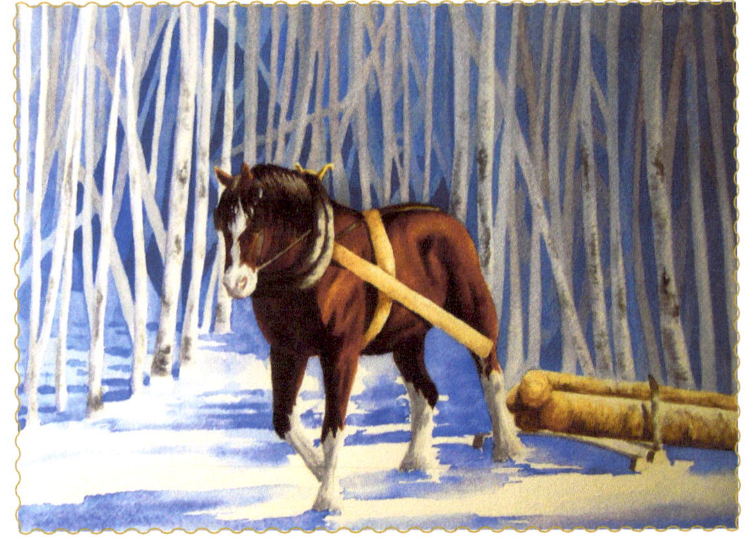

Kathryn Ragan

Every horse thinks its own pack heaviest.
Thomas Fuller, (1608-1661)

A man in passion rides a mad horse.
Benjamin Franklin, (1706-1790)

When I hear somebody talk about a horse or a cow being stupid, I figure it's a sure sign that animal has outfoxed them.

Tom Dorrance, (1910-2003)

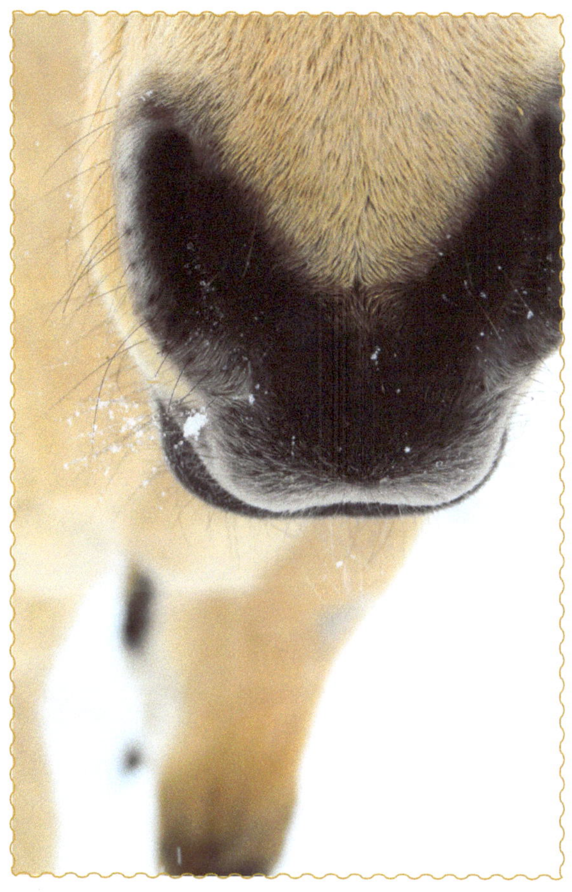

Kyleen Hafferkamp

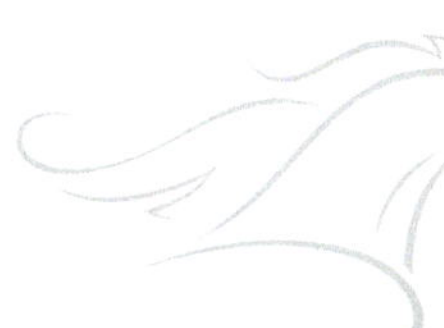

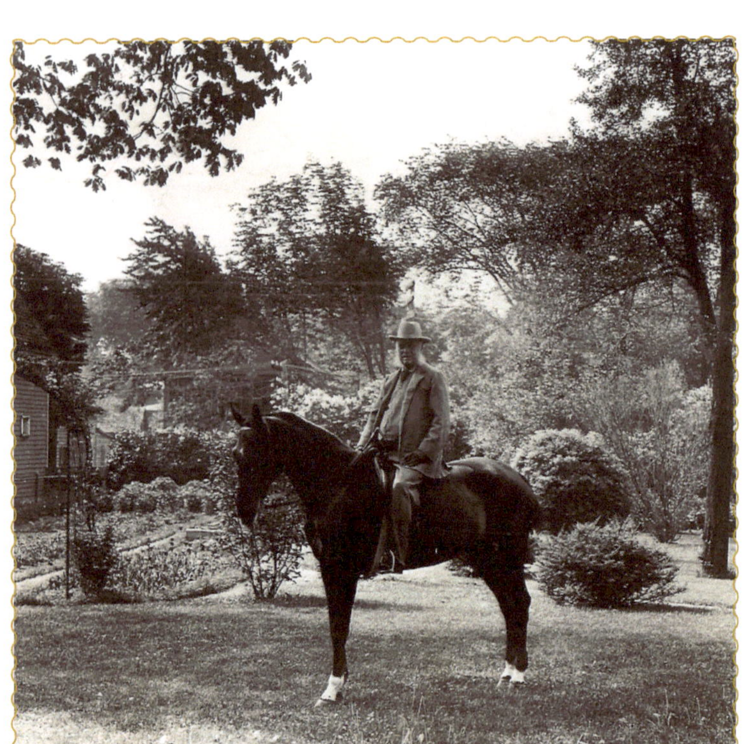

The Honorable Charles Andrews
Charles Andrews III

If you ride a horse, sit close and tight,
If you ride a man, sit easy and light.

Benjamin Franklin, (1706-1790)

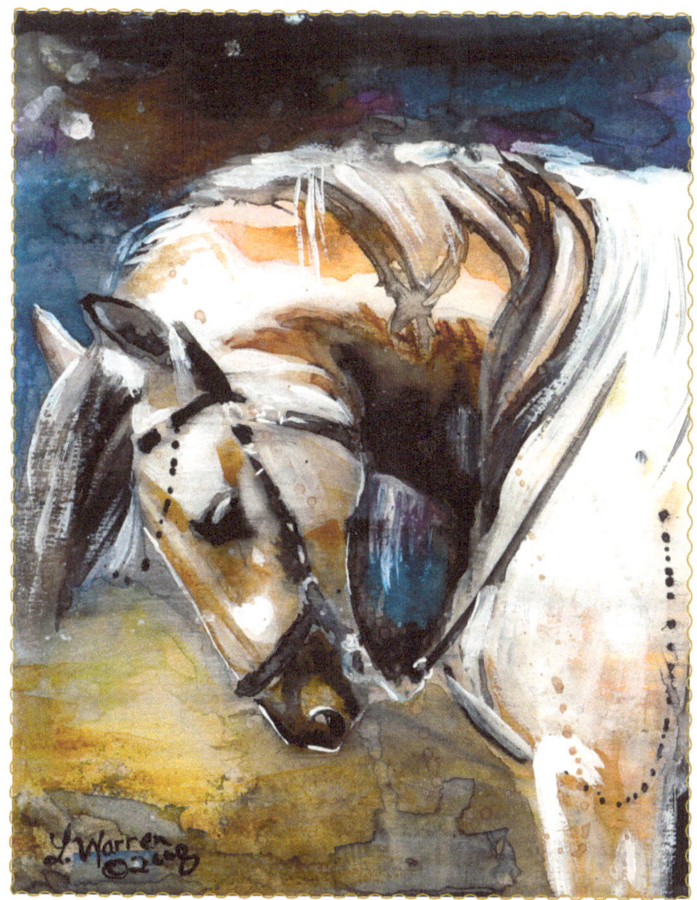

Lyndsey Warren

I speak Spanish to God, Italian to women, French to men and German to my horse.

Charles V. Holy Roman Emperor, (1500-1558)

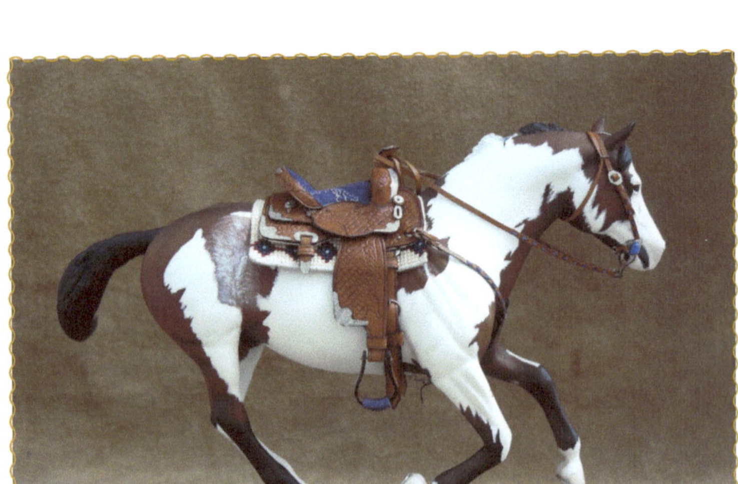

Laurence Cassin

There is something about riding down the street on a prancing horse that makes you feel like something, even when you ain't a thing.

Will Rogers, (1879-1935)

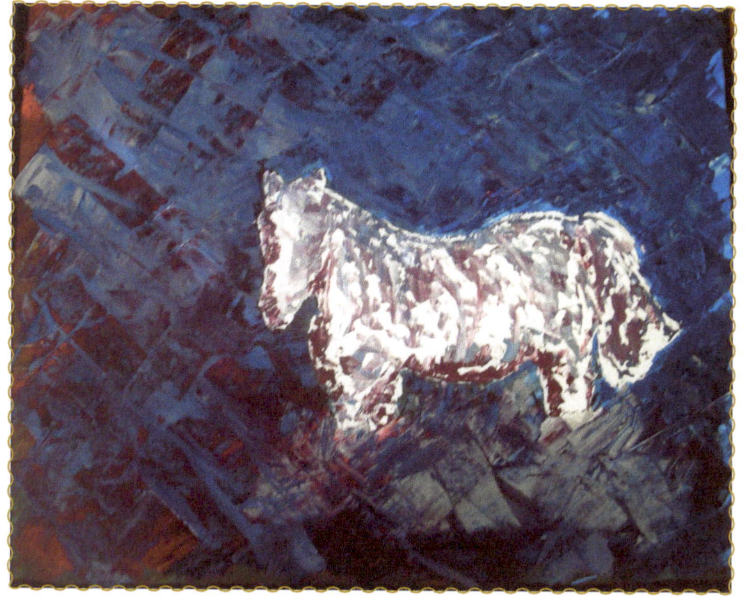

Kayla Clark

A young trooper should have an old horse.

H. G. Bohn, (1796-1884)

Time is the rider that breaks youth.

George Herbert, (1593-1633)

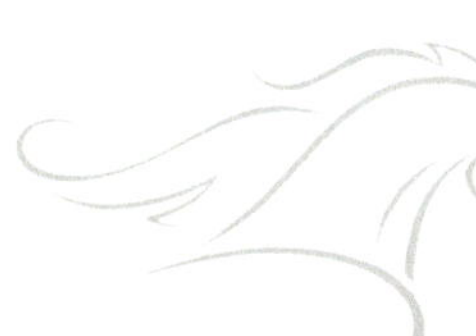

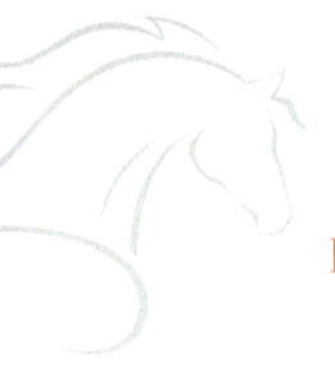

Show me a man who has no pity on his horse, and I will show you one who is a cruel husband.

George Eliot, (1819-1880)

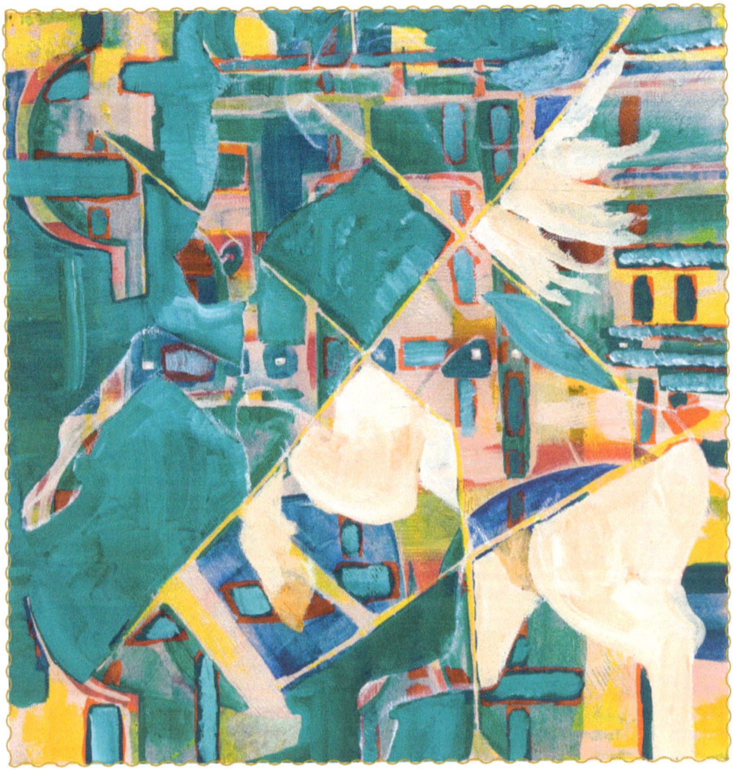

Meg Mackenzie

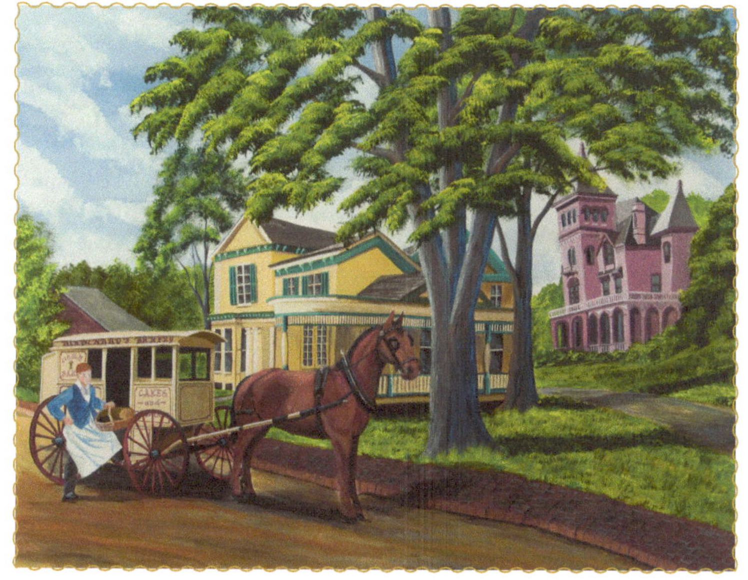

Charlotte Blanchard

The substitution of the internal combustion engine for the horse marked a very gloomy milestone in the progress of mankind.

Sir Winston Churchill, (1874-1965)

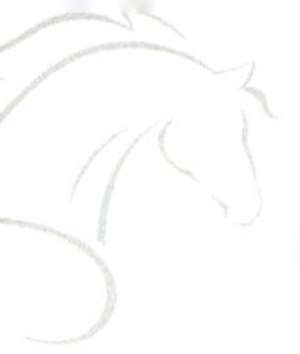

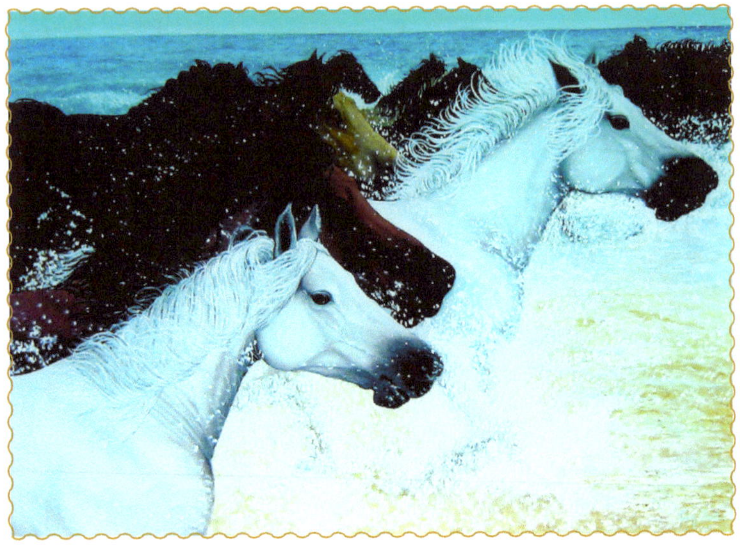

Carry Smith

It makes men imperious to sit a horse.

Oliver Wendell Holmes, Sr., (1809-1894)

Courage is being scared to death and saddling up anyways.

John Wayne, (1907-1979)

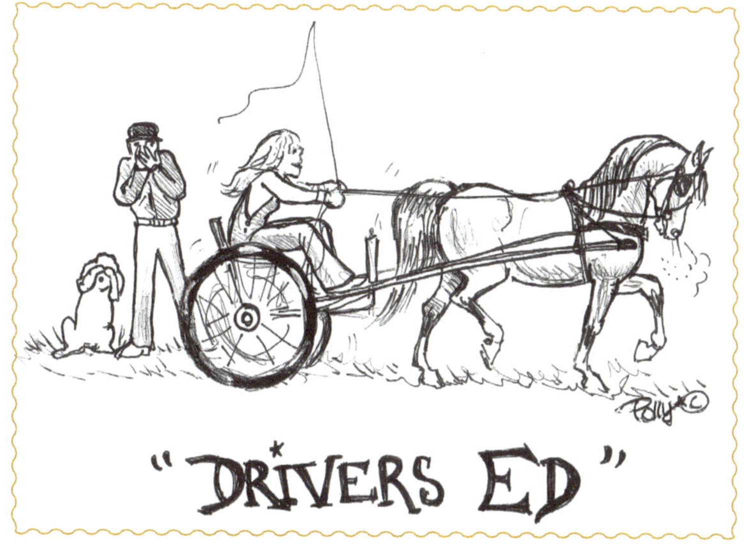

Polly Holabird

He that riseth late, must trot all day, and shall scarce overtake his business at night.

Benjamin Franklin, (1706-1790)

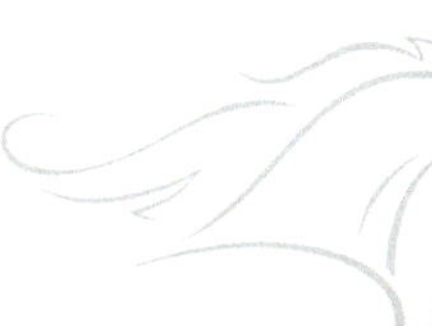

There is something about the outside of a horse that is good for the inside of a man.

Sir Winston Churchill, (1874-1965)

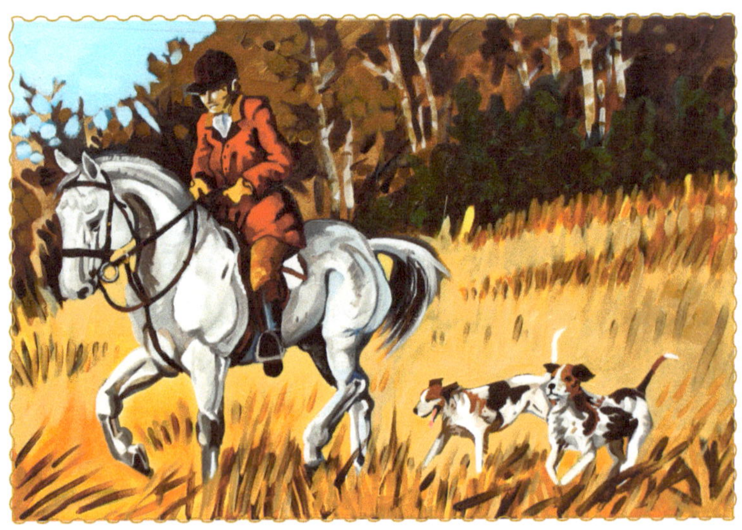

Erica Veit

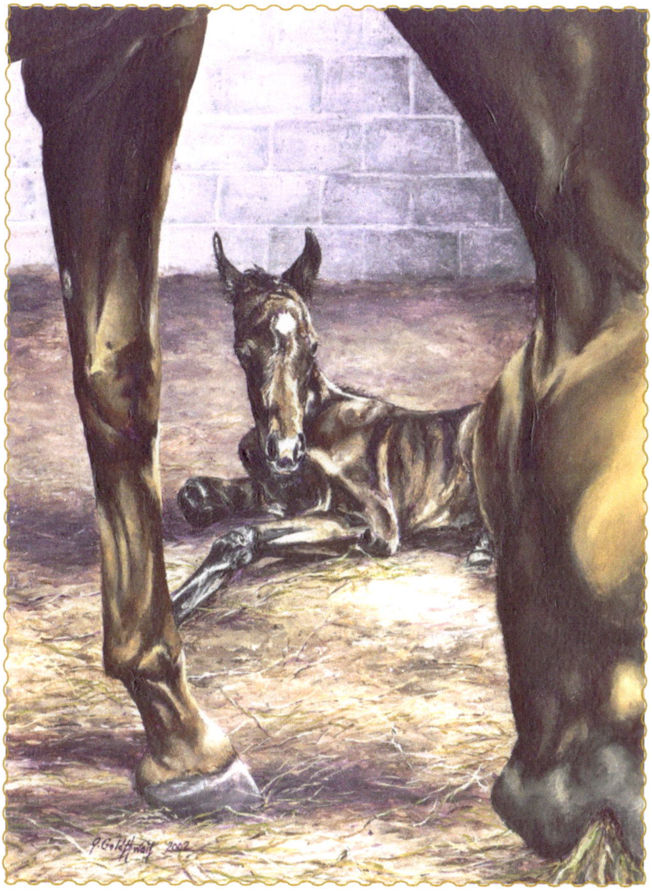

Judy Goldthwait

Men are generally more careful of the breeding of their horses and dogs than of their children.

William Penn, (1644-1718)

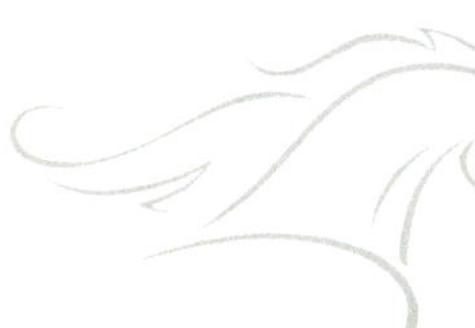

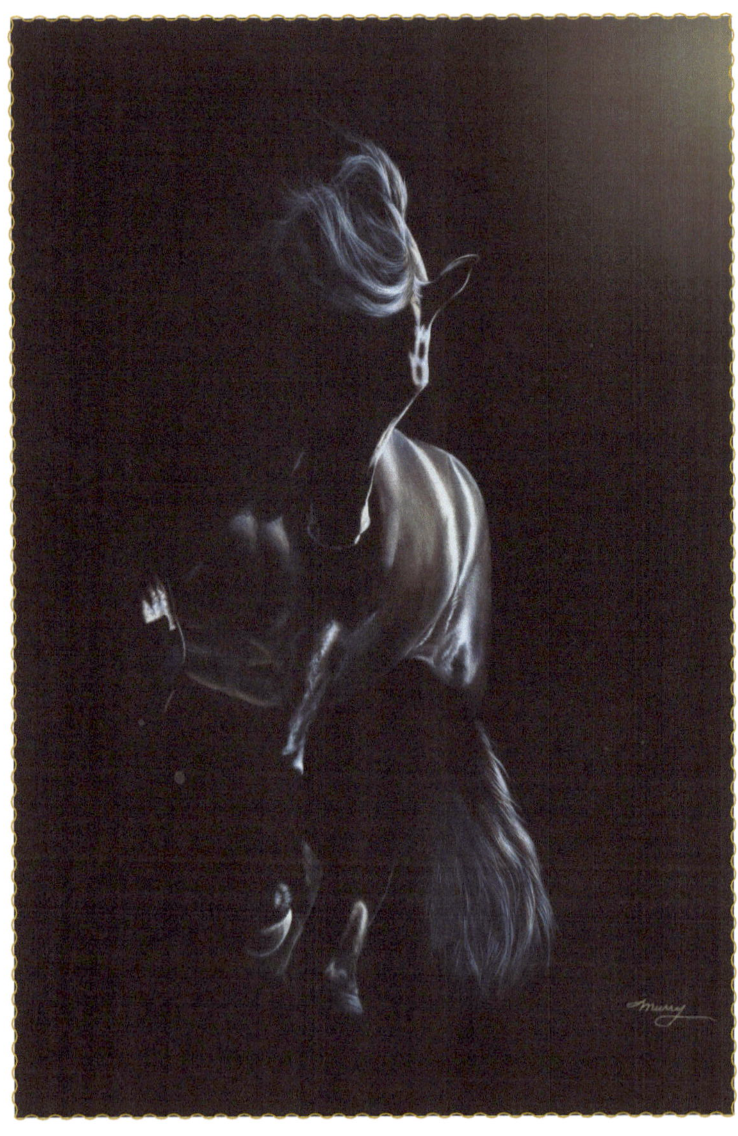

Dee Dee Murry

"The Midnight Ride of Paul Revere"

On the opposite shore walked Paul Revere.
Now he patted his horse's side,
Now he gazed at the landscape far and near,
Then, impetuous, stamped the earth,
And turned and tightened his saddle girth . . .
He springs to the saddle, the bridle he turns,
But lingers and gazes, till full on his sight
A second lamp in the belfry burns.

Henry Wadsworth Longfellow, (1807-1882)

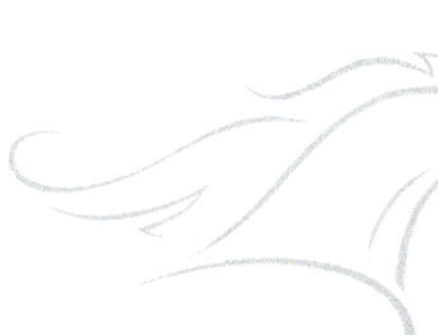

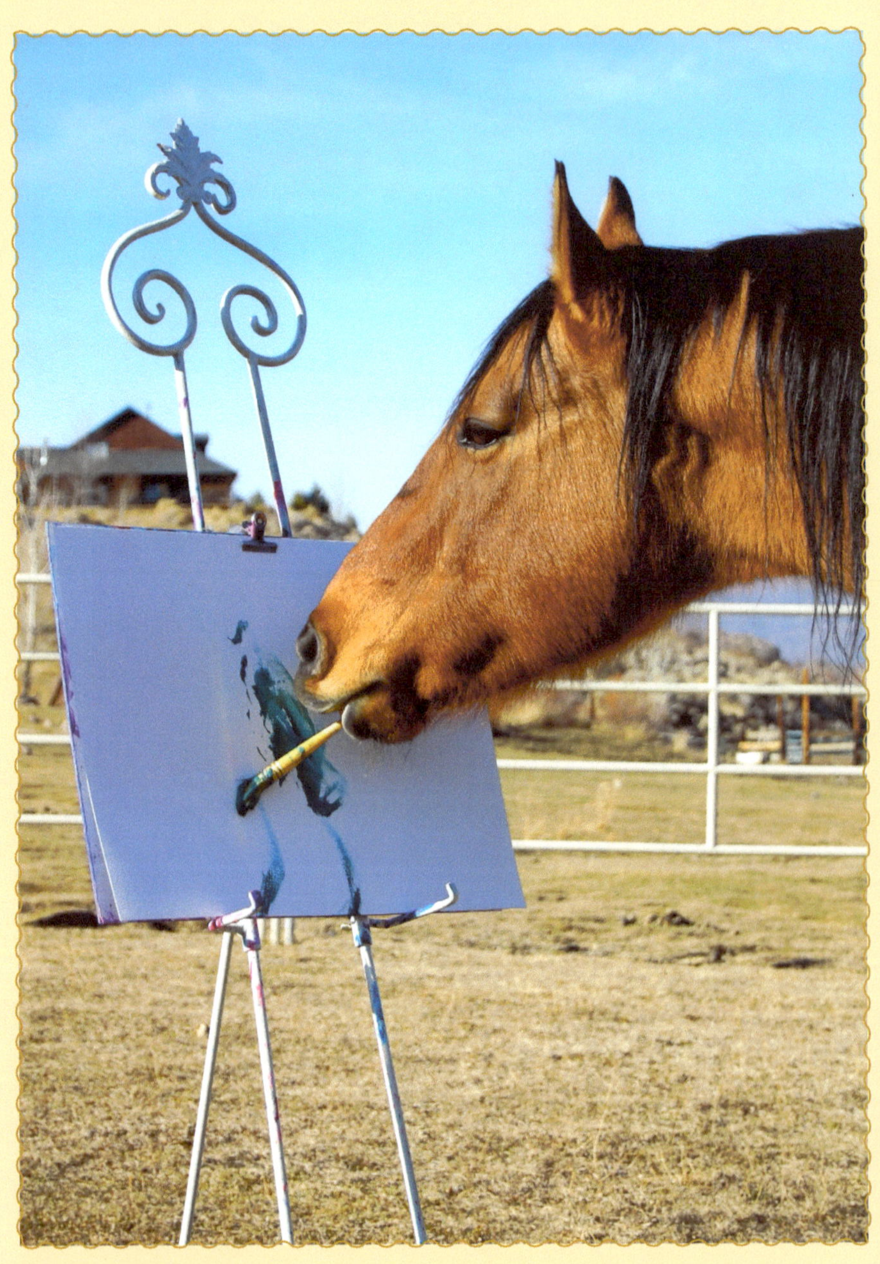

Cholla Chambers

CHAPTER 5

Cholla

When I decided to do this book featuring equine artists, I never expected to have an actual horse artist. But what a wonderful surprise! I guess it confirms what we all know, horses are amazing. Cholla Chambers is an international Artist. He has won 2 Honorable Mention Art Awards, one from Venice, Italy where he was also given a solo show in 2009. His art has shown in galleries across the USA including NYC, Vegas, Reno, and San Francisco. His art has been described as having "the fire of Pollock" and "the fixed gaze of Resnick".

The image of the big red bucking horse in Cholla's "The Big Red Buck", is quite obvious. Cholla was not trained to paint and he holds his brush with his teeth, and, oh yes, Cholla is a horse.

You can learn more about Cholla and his art at

www.ArtistisaHorse.com

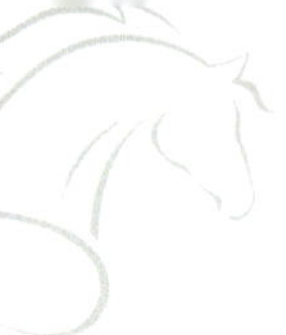

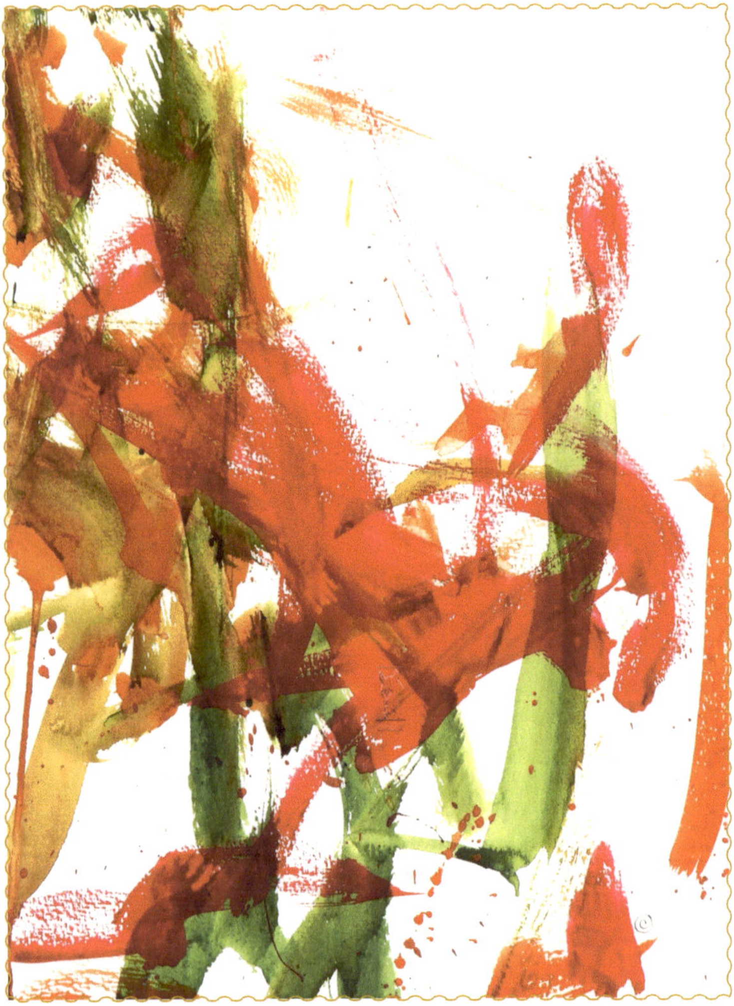

Big Red Buck, Cholla Chambers

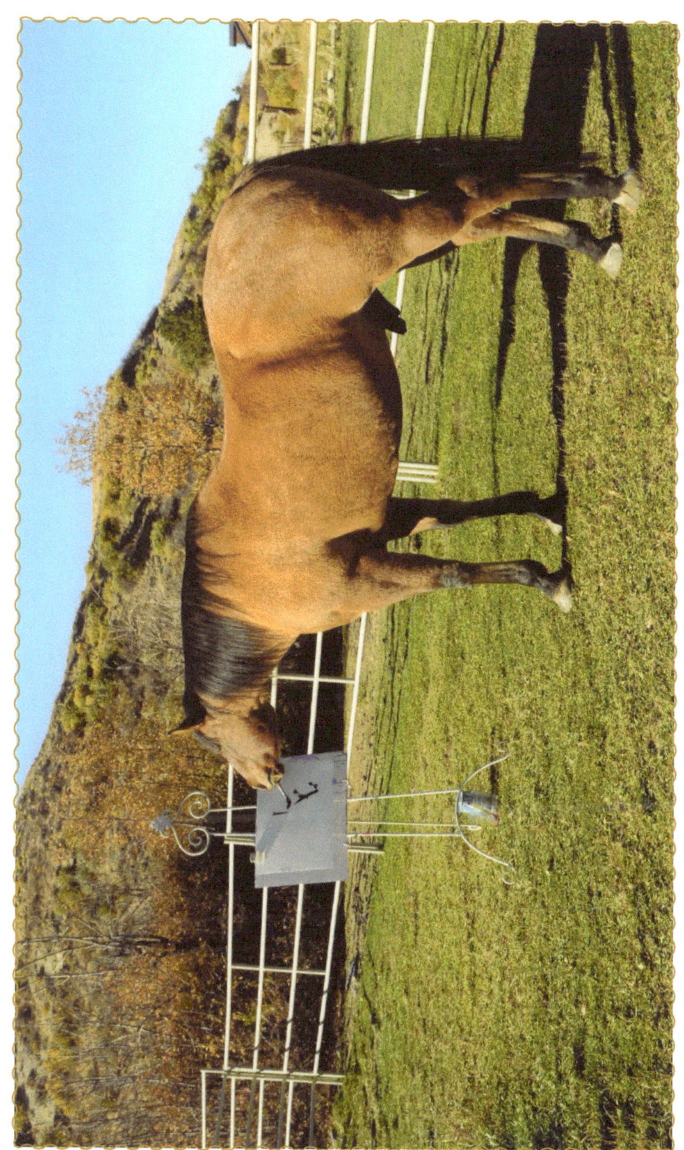

Cholla Chambers

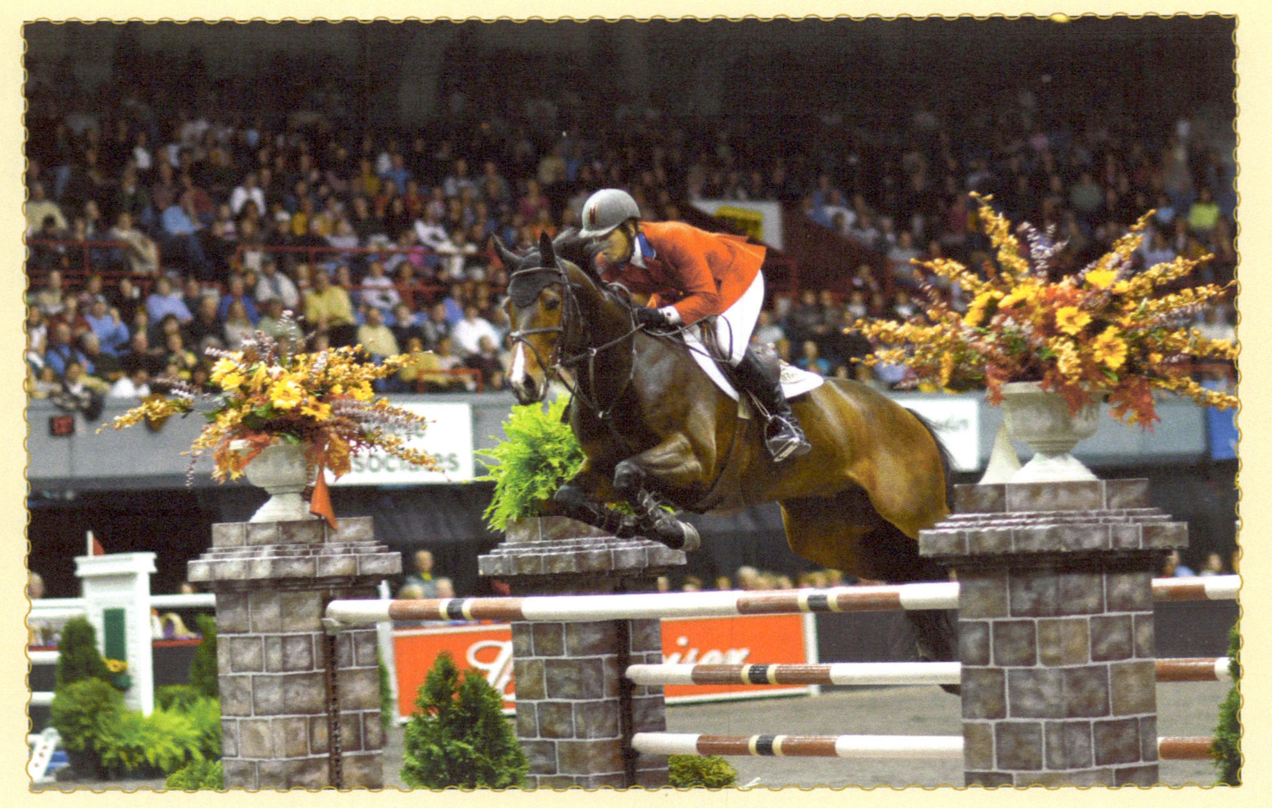

Olympic Gold Medallist Beezie Madden on Authentic

CHAPTER 6

Competing

There is something about jumping a horse over a fence, something that makes you feel good. Perhaps it's the risk, the gamble. In any event it's a thing I need.

William Faulkner, (1897-1962)

There are fools, damn fools, and those who remount in a steeplechase.

Bill Whitbread, (1930-2004)

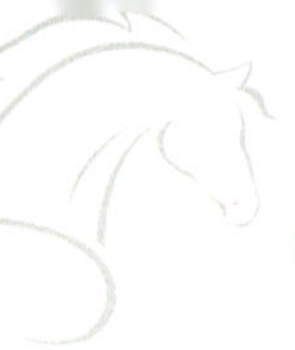

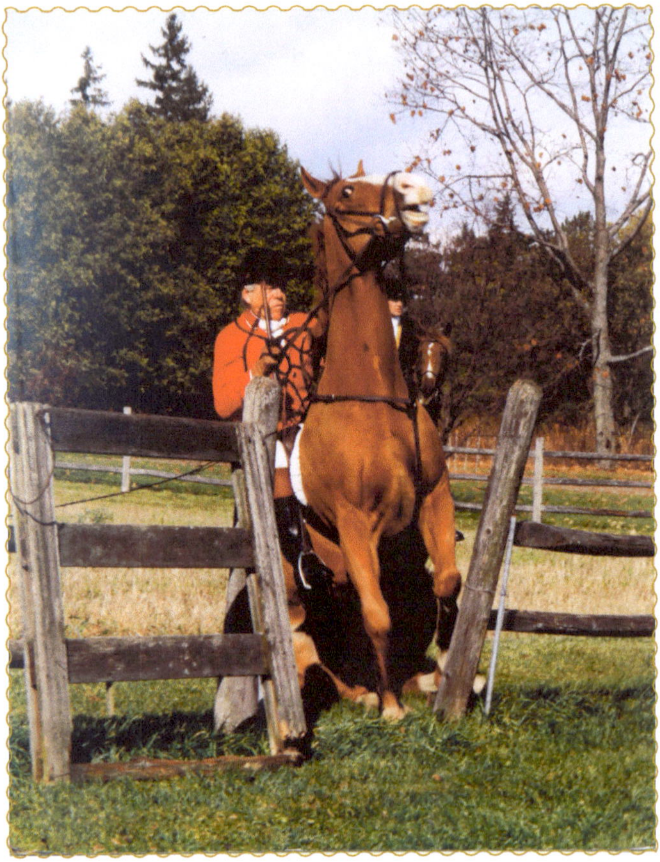

Gene Gissin

A horse which stops dead just before a jump and thus propels its rider into a graceful arc provides a splendid excuse for general merriment.

Prince Philip, Duke of Edinburgh, (b. 1921)

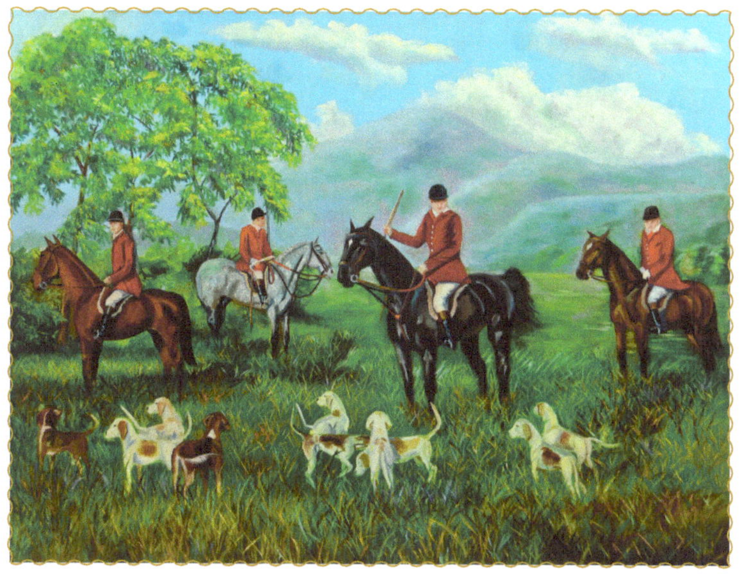

Charlotte Blanchard

Let the best horse leap the hedge first.

Thomas Fuller, (1608-1661)

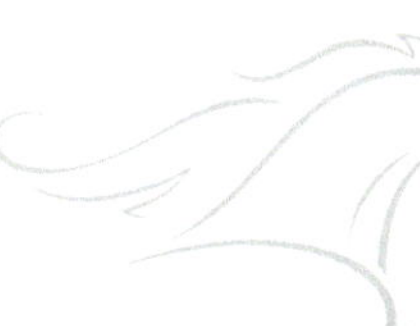

There are only two classes of good society in England, the equestrian classes and the neurotic classes. It isn't mere convention, everybody can see that the people who hunt are the right people and the people who don't are the wrong ones.

George Bernard Shaw, (1856-1950)

Twas the sound of his horn called me from my bed,
And the cry of his hounds has me oft-times led,
For Peel's View-halloo would waken the dead,
Or a fox from his lair in the morning.

John Woodcock Graves, (1795-1886)

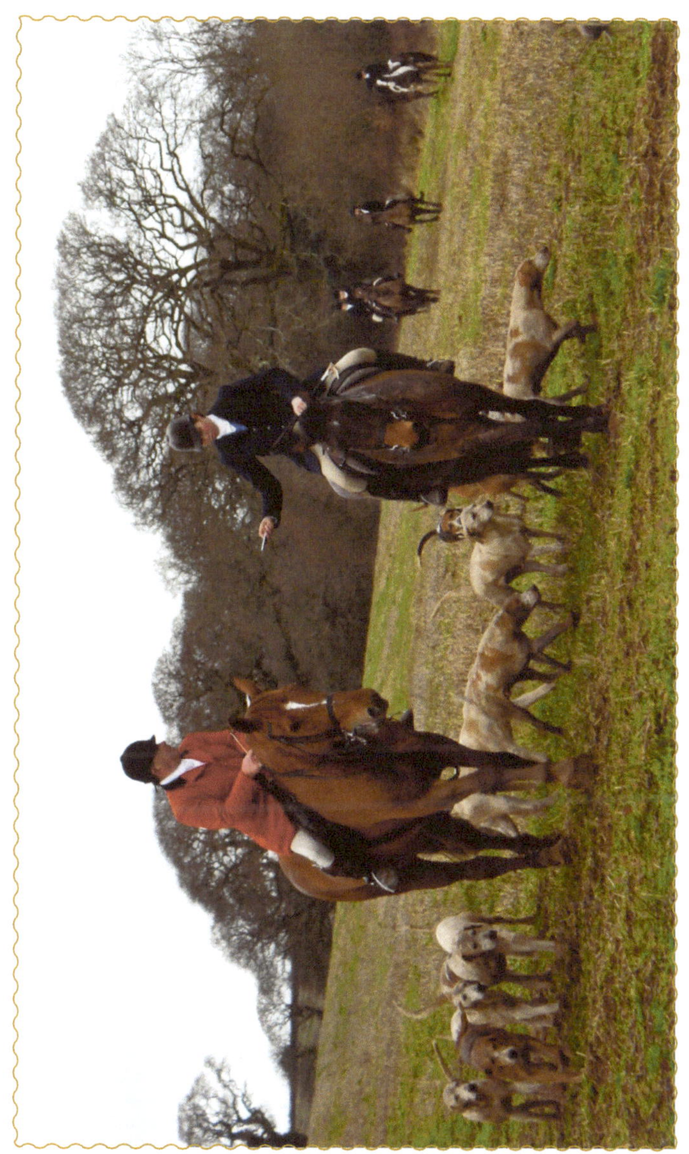

Hannah Tippett

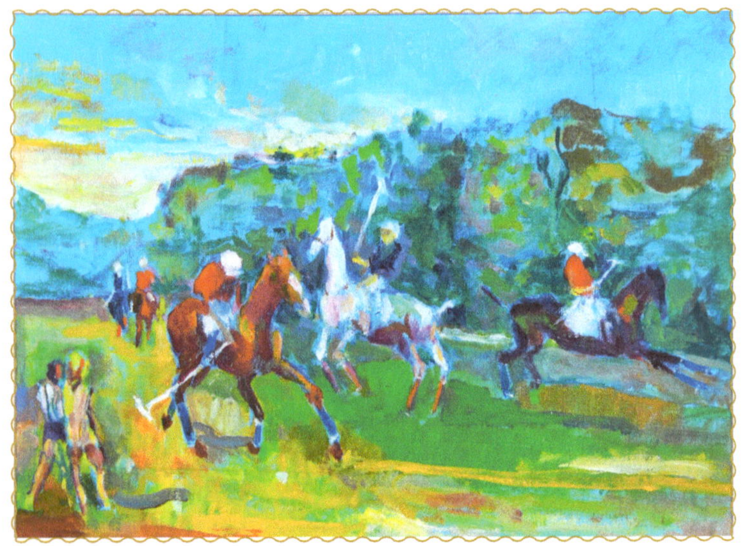

Richard Hubbard

O the horseman's and horsewoman's joys!
The saddle, the gallop, the pressure upon the seat,
the cool gurgling by the ears and hair.

Walt Whitman, (1819-1892)

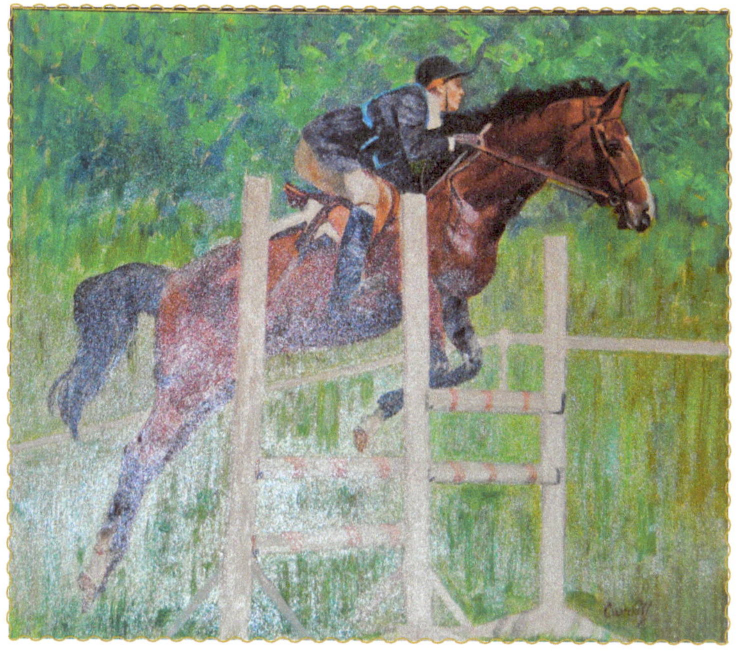

Gigi Redmond

Nothing can match the thrill of riding good horses at speed over fences—nothing! I don't see that courage has anything to do with it. It's simply a job we all enjoy doing.

Bob Champion, (b. 1948)

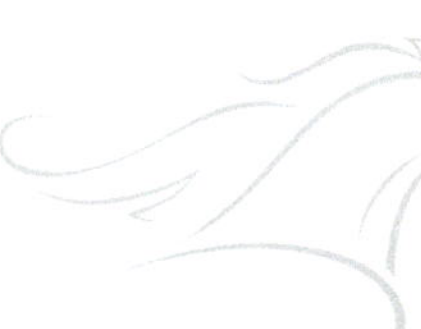

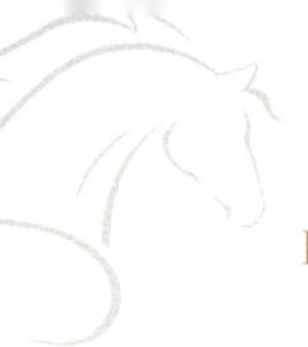

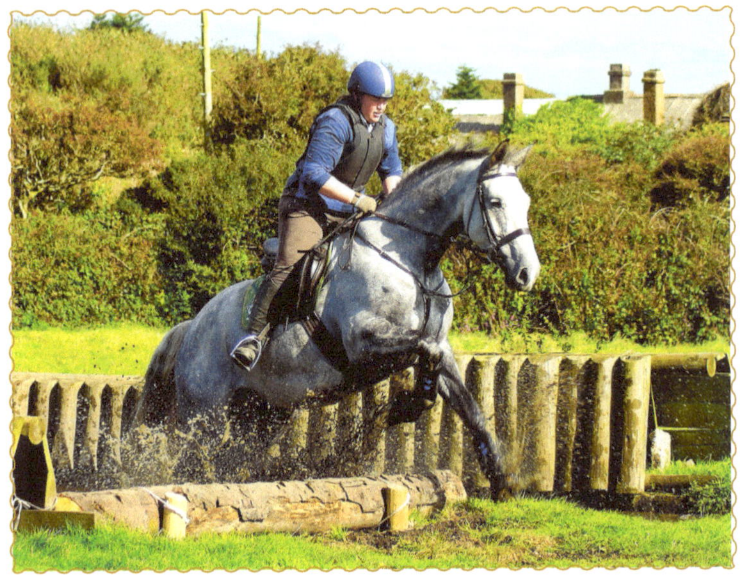

Hannah Tippett

Each handicap is like a hurdle in a steeplechase, and when you ride up to it, if you throw your heart over, the horse will go along, too.

Lawrence Bixby, (1895-1982)

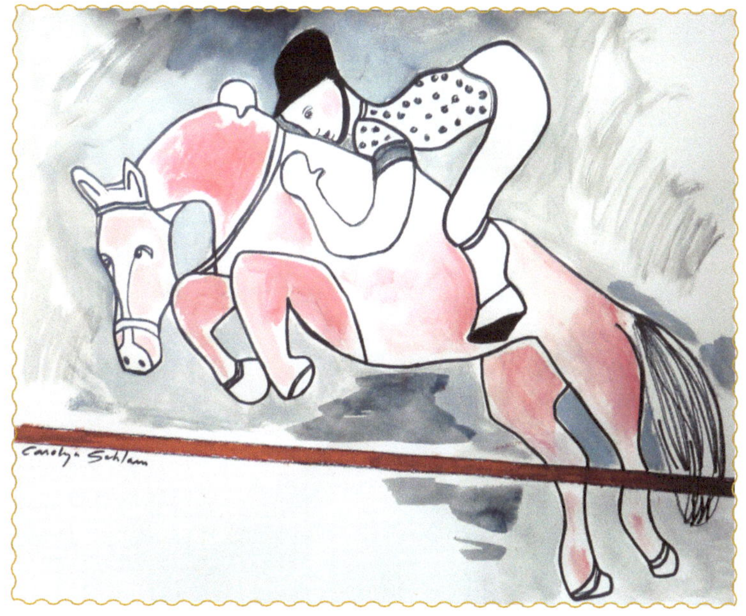

Carolyn Schlam

[Steeplechasing] is one of the real sports that's left, isn't it? A bit of danger, a bit of excitement and the horses—the best thing in the world.

Queen Elizabeth, the Queen Mother,
(1900-2002)

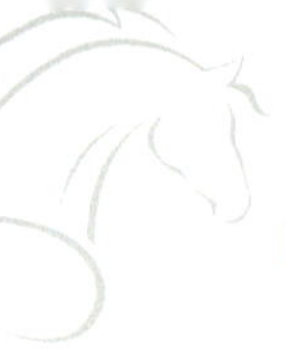

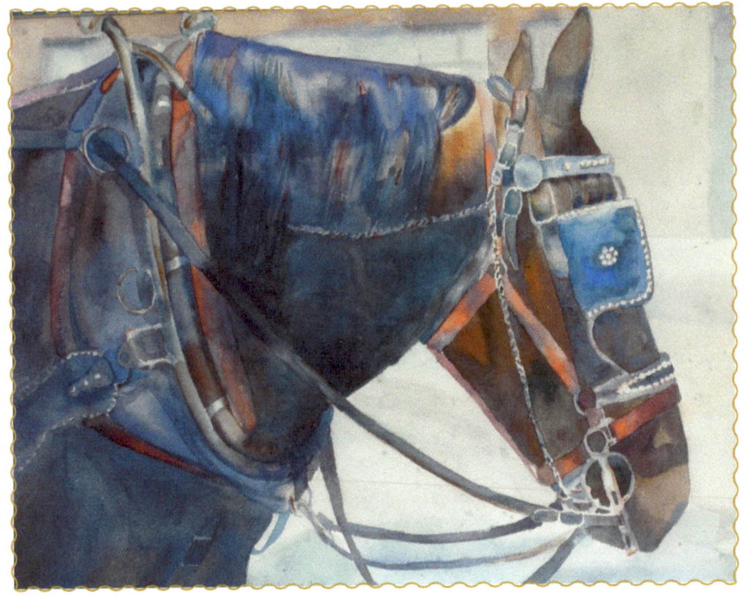

Marika Anderson

You never know how a horse will pull until you hook him to a heavy load.

Paul Bryant, (1913-1983)

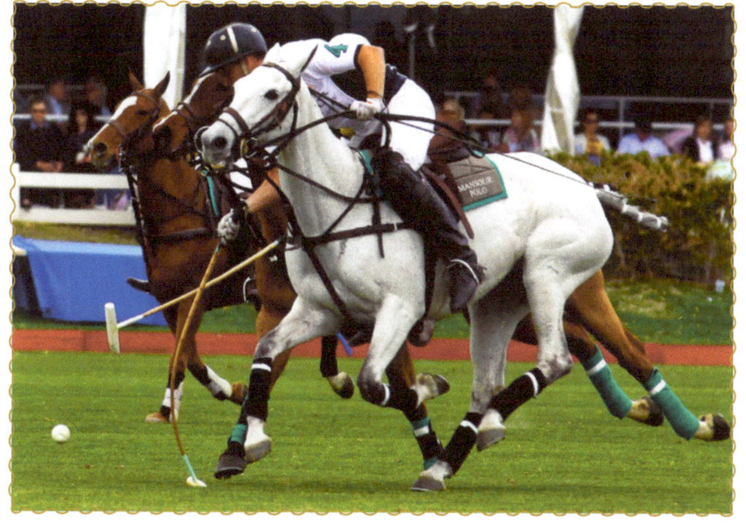

Romain Brumby

Playing polo is like trying to play golf during an earthquake.

Sylvester Stallone, (b. 1946)

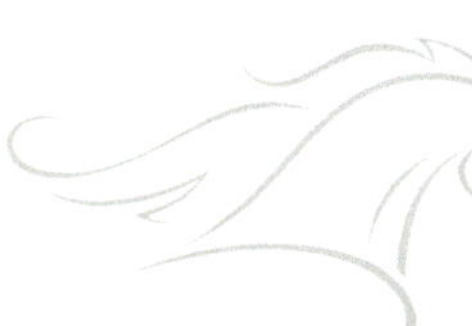

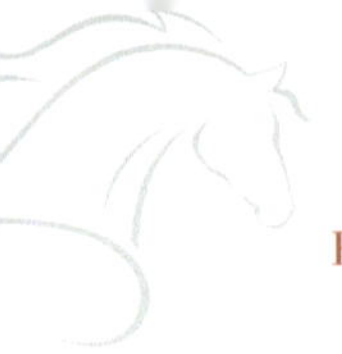

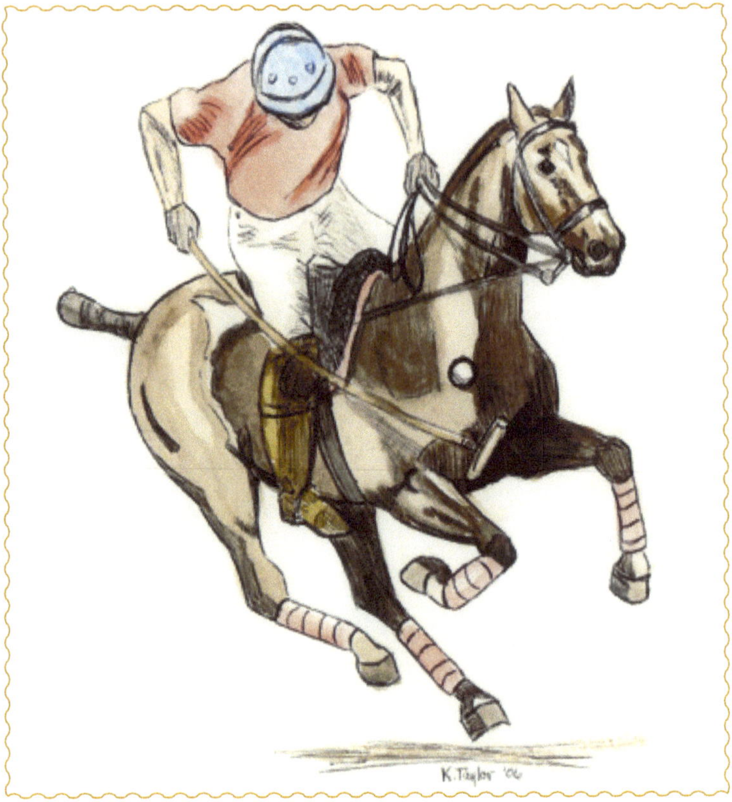

Kristin Taylor

After seeing kids play polo against big guys, it only shows that horses are the greatest equalizer in the world. No matter what you weigh, the little fellow is your equal on a horse.

Will Rogers, (1879-1935)

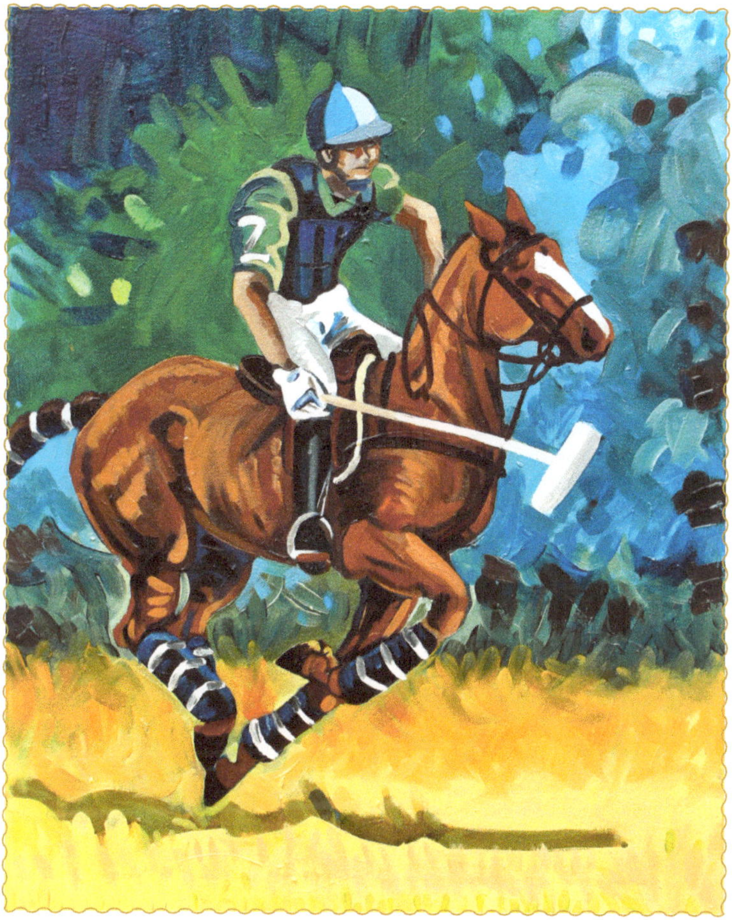

Erica Veit

A polo handicap is a person's ticket to the world.

Sir Winston Churchill, (1874-1965)

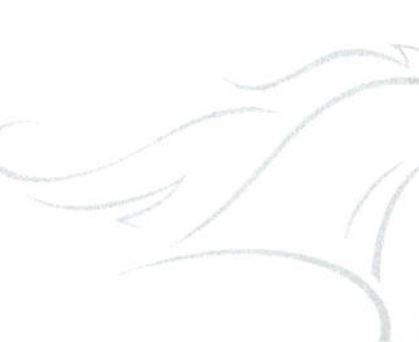

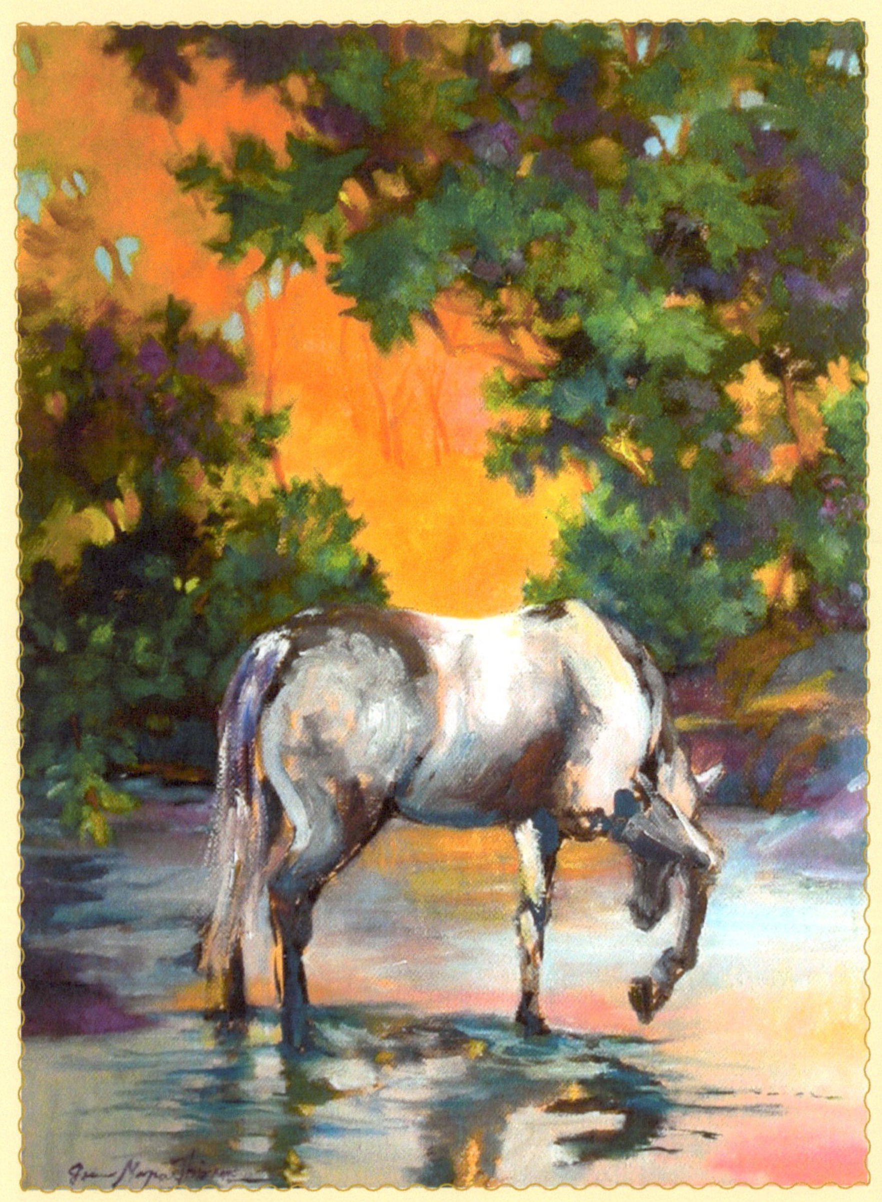

Jeanne M. Thieme

CHAPTER 7

Ancient Wisdom

People then, are not friend to horses unless their horses love them in return.

Plato, (428/427 B.C.-348/347 B.C.)

A horse is a thing of such beauty . . . none will tire of looking at him as long as he displays himself in his splendor.

Xenophon, (430 B.C.-354 B.C.)

A horse! A horse! My kingdom for a horse!

William Shakespeare, (1564-1616)

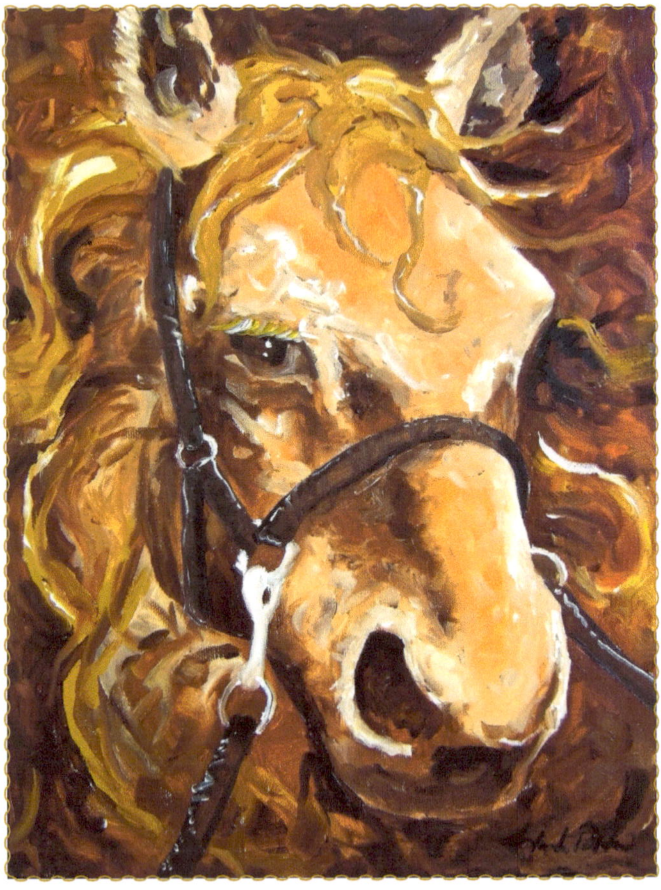

Joseph Palotas

Old minds are like old horses; you must exercise them if you wish to keep them in working order.

John Adams, (1797-1801)

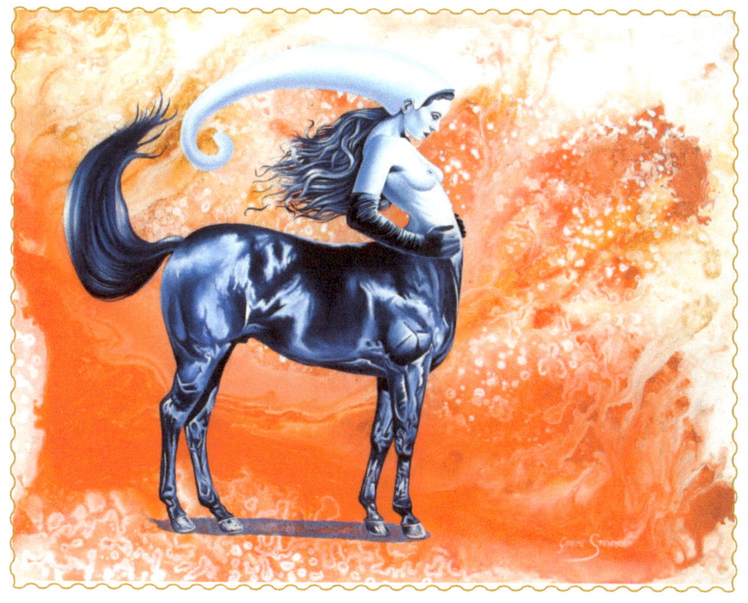

Graeme Stevenson

No gymnastics could be better or harder exercise, and this and the art of riding, are of all the arts the most befitting a free man.

Plato, (428/427 B.C.-348/347 B.C.)

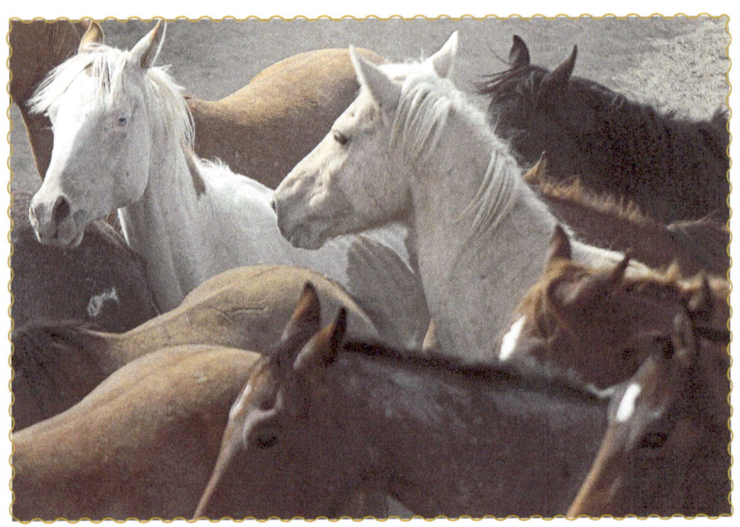

Jackie Cercek

Their [the Tartars'] horses are so well broken-in to quick changes of movement, that upon the signal given, they instantly turn in every direction, and by these rapid maneuvers many victories have been won.

Marco Polo, (1254-1324)

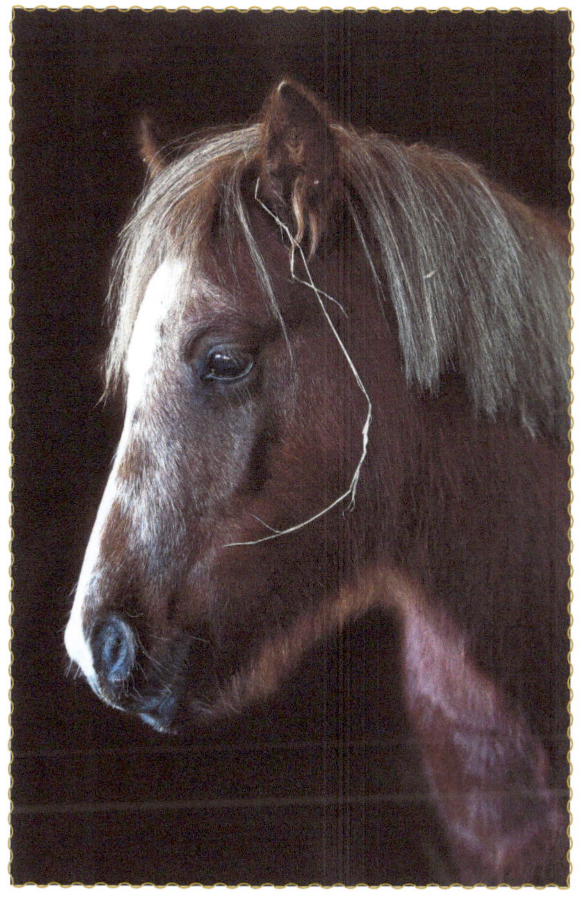

Sian Lewis

It is also good to pet the beast while he eats so that he will relax.

Marcus Aurelius, (121-180)

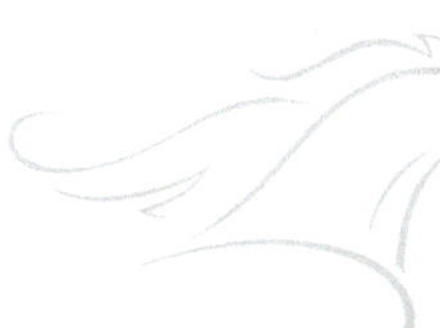

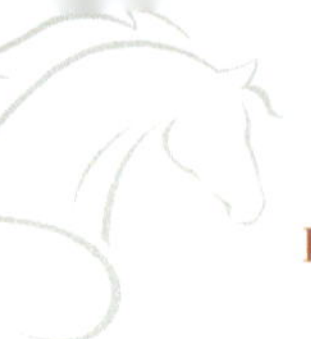

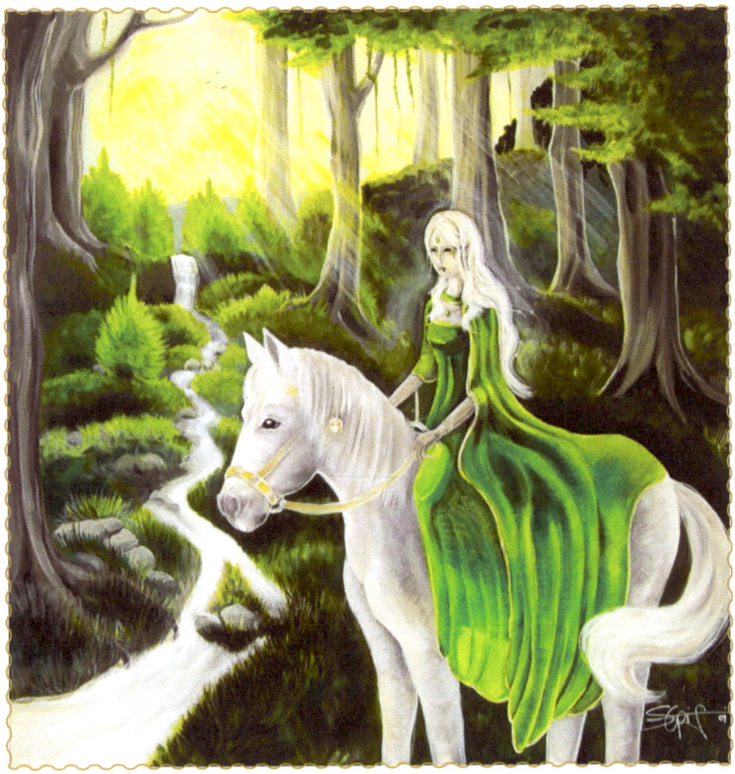

Sabrina Epifani

We judge a horse not only by its pace on a race-course, but also by its walk, nay, when resting in its stable.

Michel de Montaigne, (1533-1592)

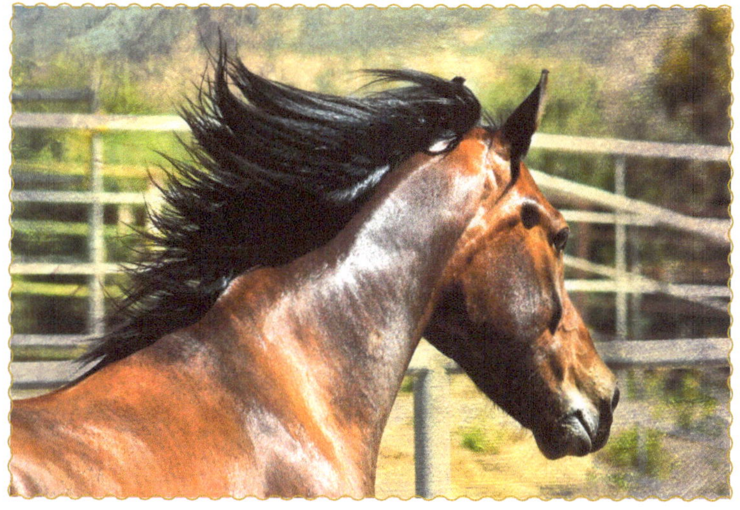

Susan Kordish

The spirited horse, which will try to win the race of its own accord, will run even faster if encouraged.

Ovid, (43 B.C.-A.D. 17/18)

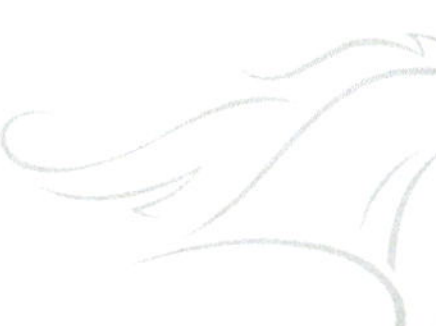

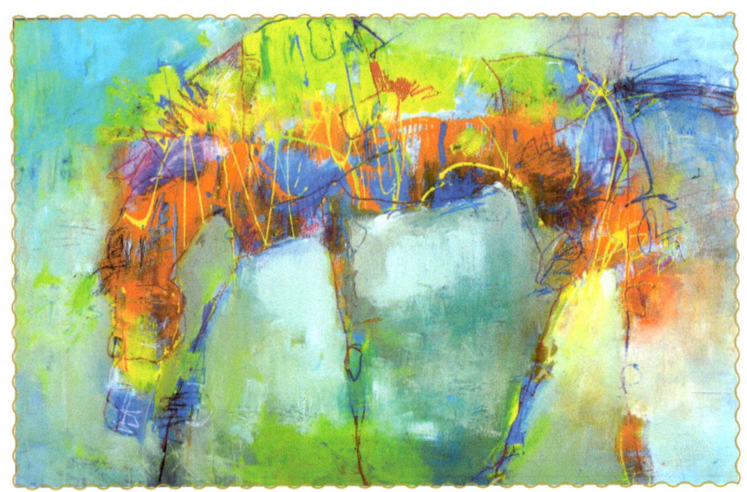

Melissa Mason

A little neglect may breed mischief: for want of a nail the shoe was lost, for want of a shoe the horse was lost, and for want of a horse the rider was lost.

Benjamin Franklin, (1706-1790)

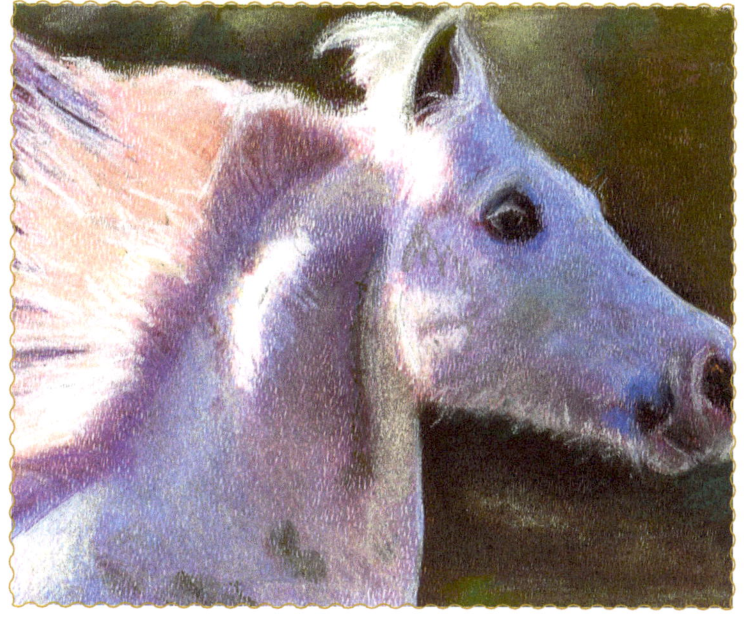

Karen Travis

Look, what a horse should have he did not lack,
Save a proud rider on so proud a back.

William Shakespeare, (1564-1616)

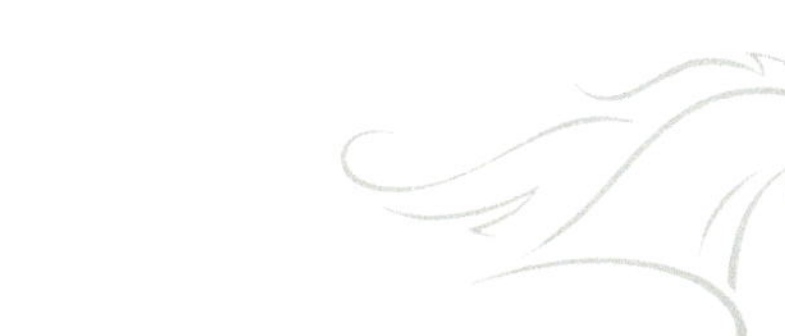

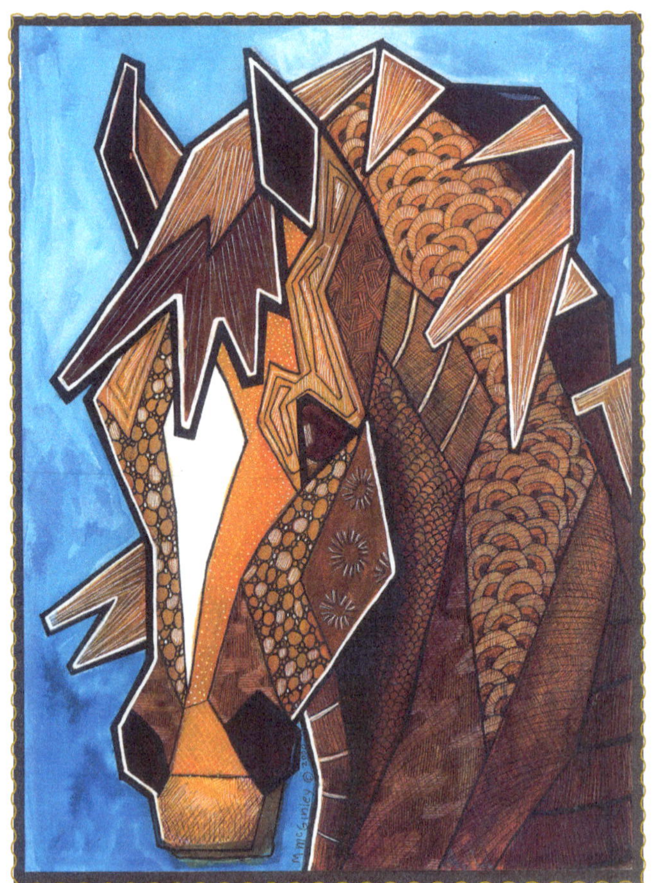

Marge McGinley

There is no need of spurs when a horse is running away.

Publilius Syrus, (1st Century B.C.)

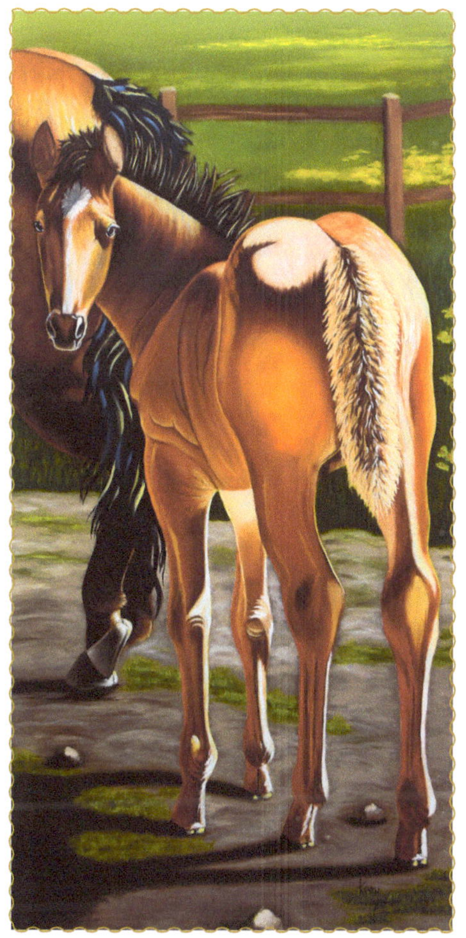

Kary Kidder

Nothing made the horse so fat as the king's eye.

Plutarch, (46-120)

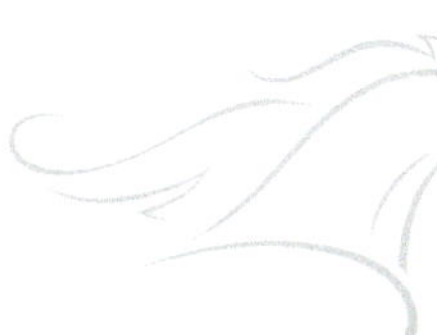

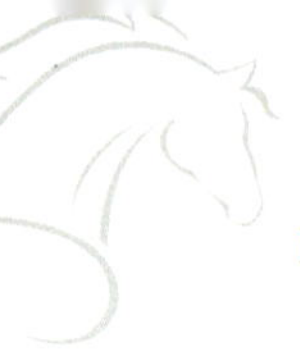

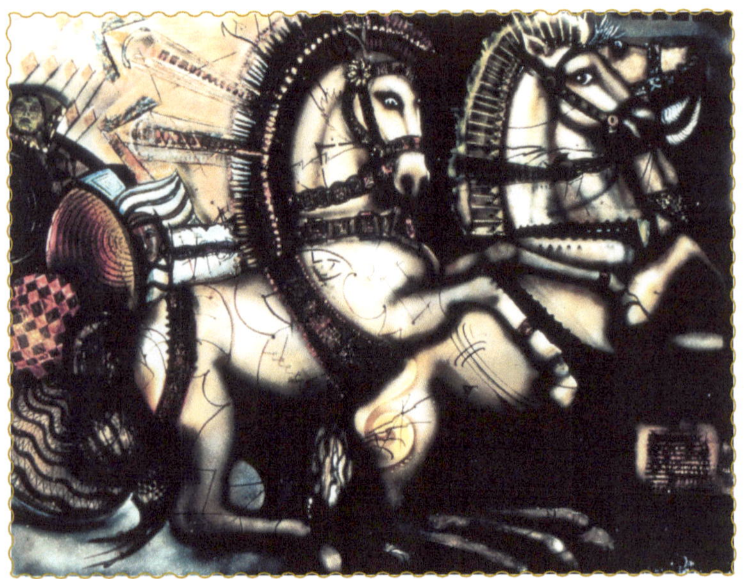

Ione Citrin

The horses of Achilles stood apart from their battle weeping, because they had learned that their charioteer had fallen in the dust by the hand of man-slaying Hector . . .

Homer, The Iliad, (8th Century B.C.)

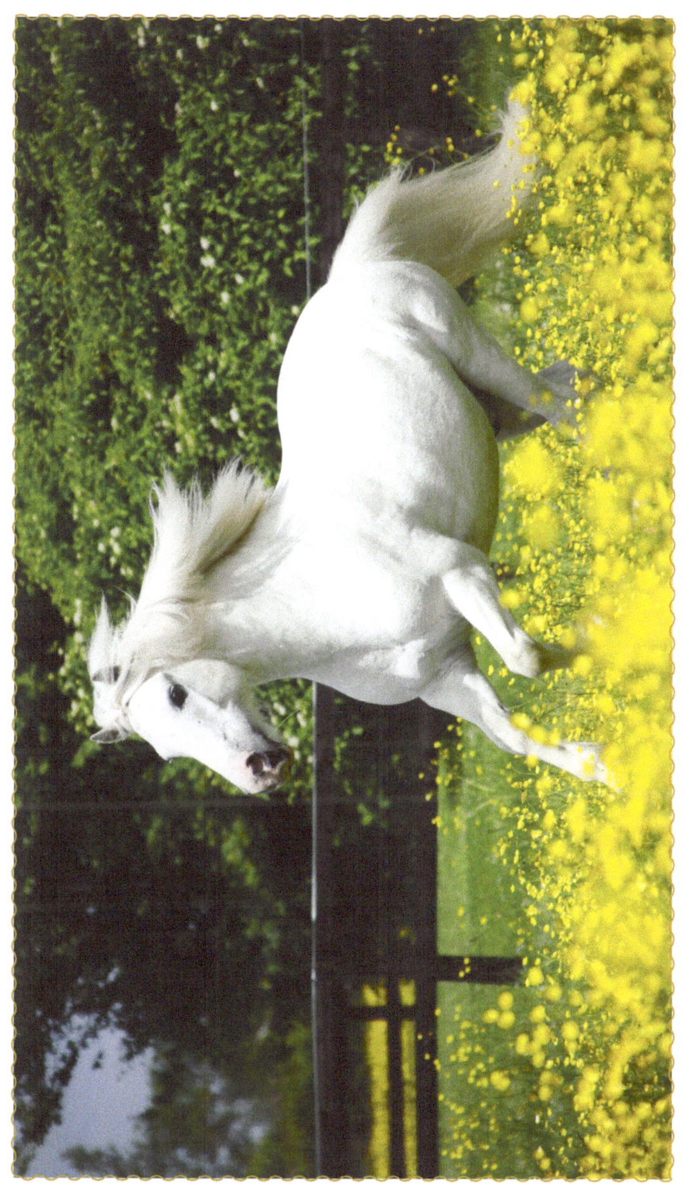

Christian Lampert-Sharp

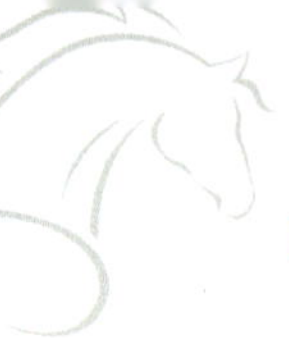

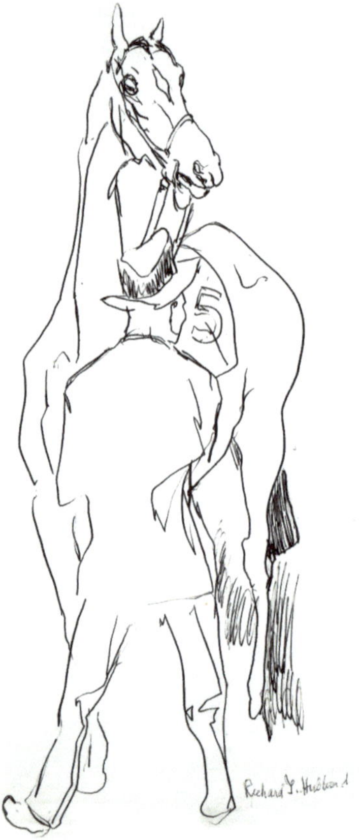

Richard Hubbard

It is the seat on a horse that makes the difference between a groom and a gentleman.

Miguel de Cervantes, (1547-1616)

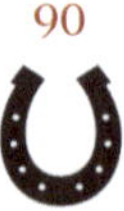

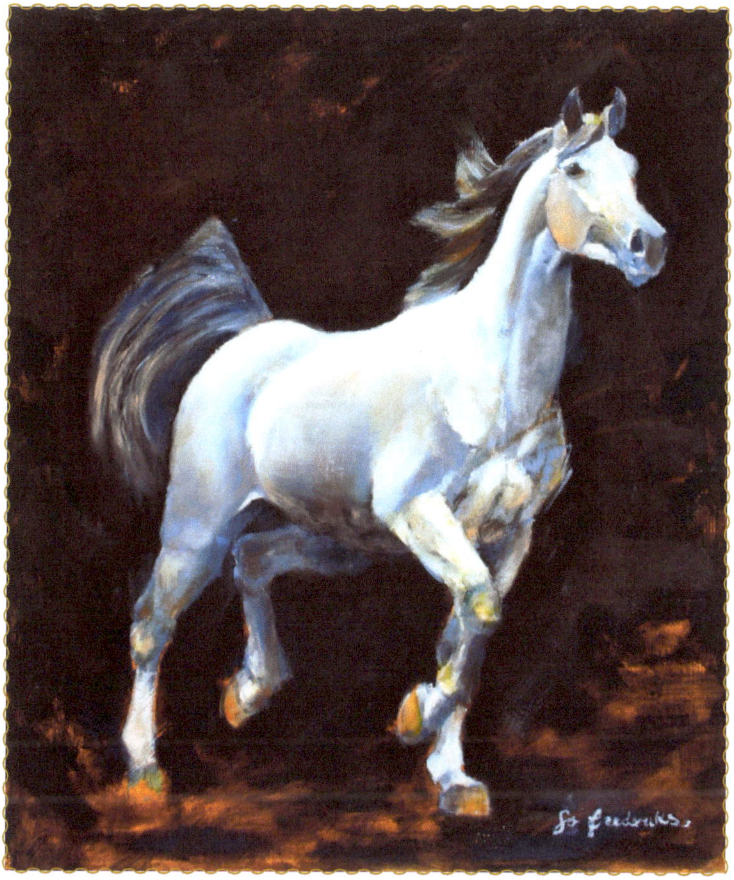

Jo Frederiks

But he, mighty man, lay mightily in the whirl of dust, forgetful of his horsemanship.

Homer, (8th Century B.C.)

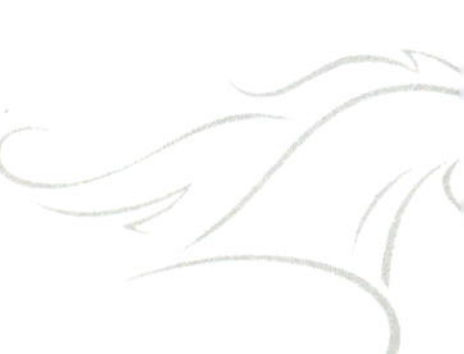

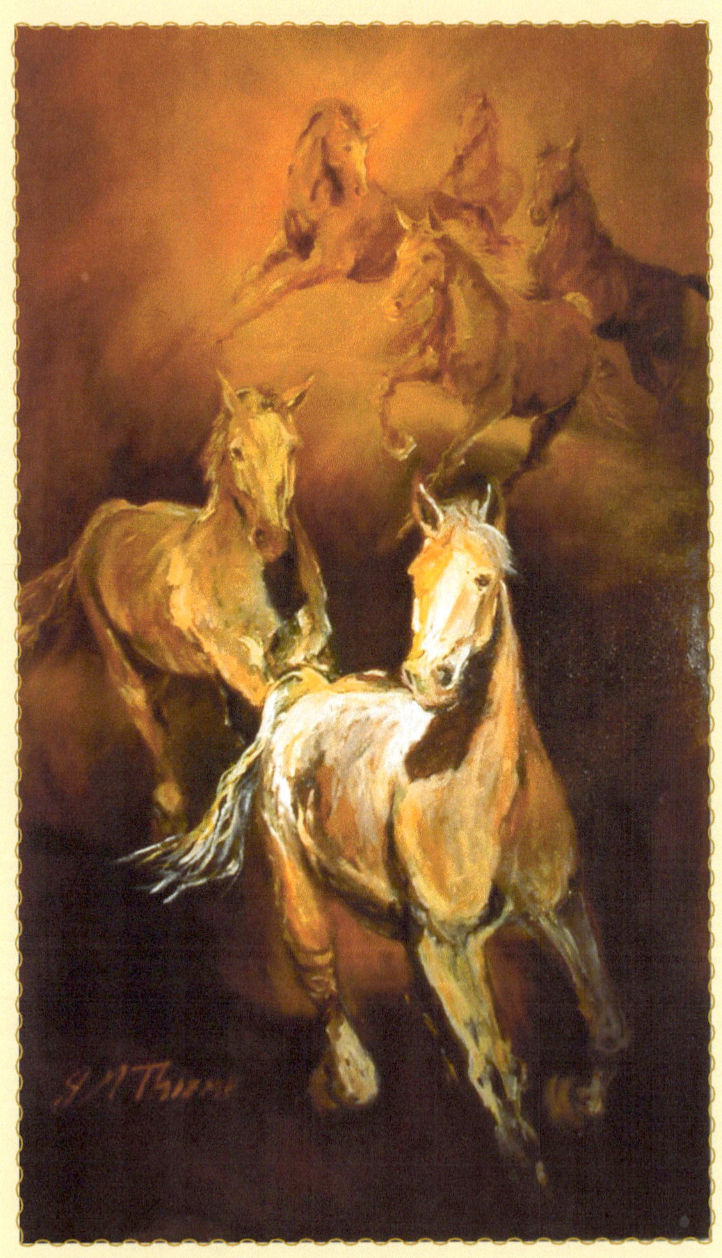

Jeanne M. Thieme

CHAPTER 8

Training & Handling

You can't control a young horse unless you can control yourself.

Lincoln Steffans, (1866-1936)

Spur not an unbroken horse.

Sir Walter Scott, (1771-1823)

The horse thinks one thing and he who saddles him another.

Benjamin Franklin, (1706-1790)

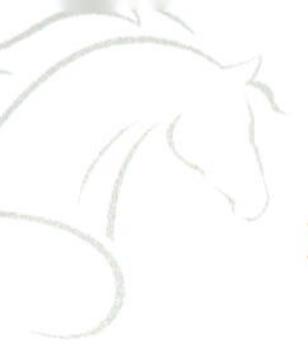

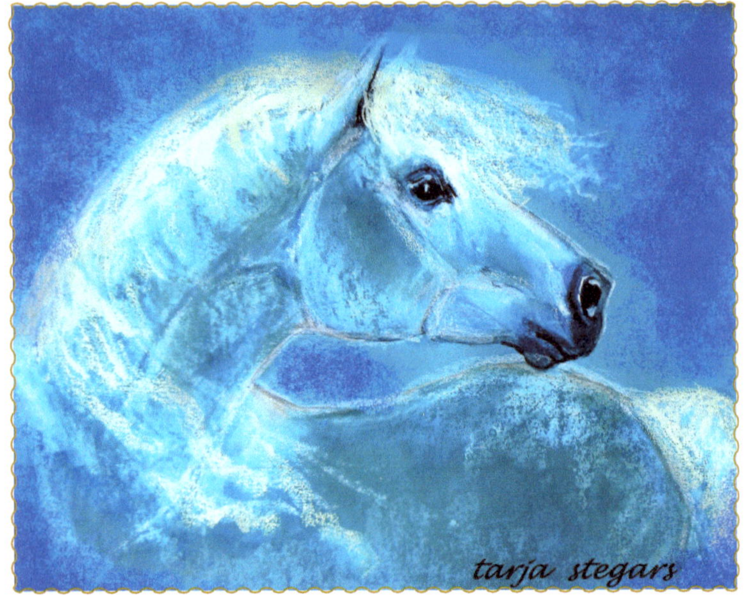

Tarja Stegars

The wildest colts make the best horses.

Plutarch, (46-120)

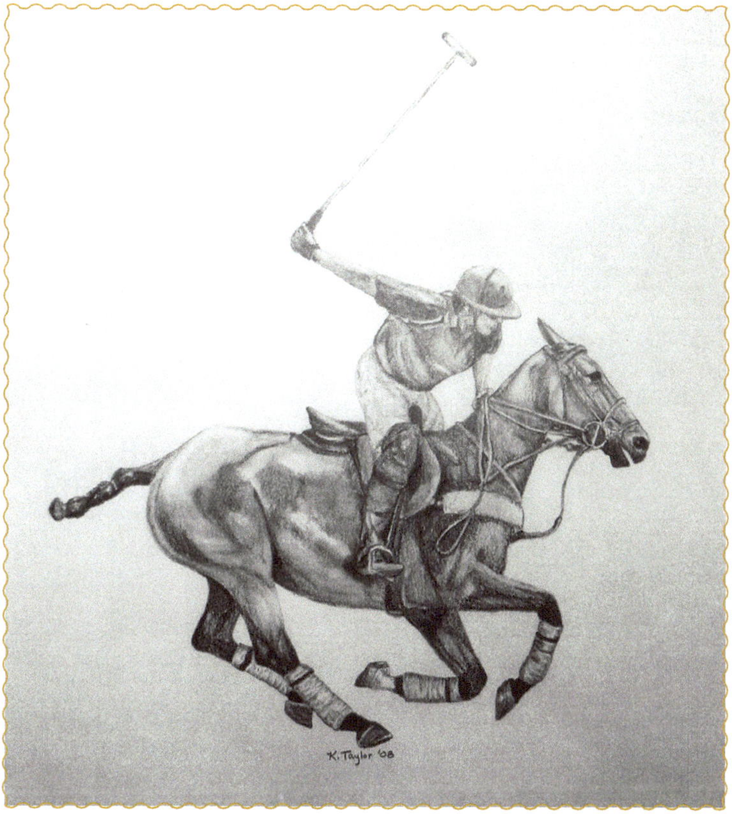

Kristin Taylor

A horse can be made to do almost anything if his master has intelligence enough to let him know what is required.

Ulysses S. Grant, (1822-1885)

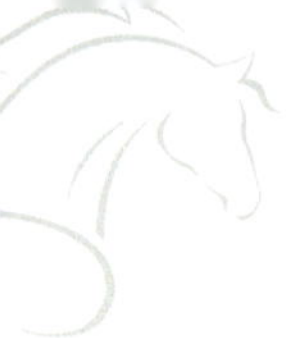

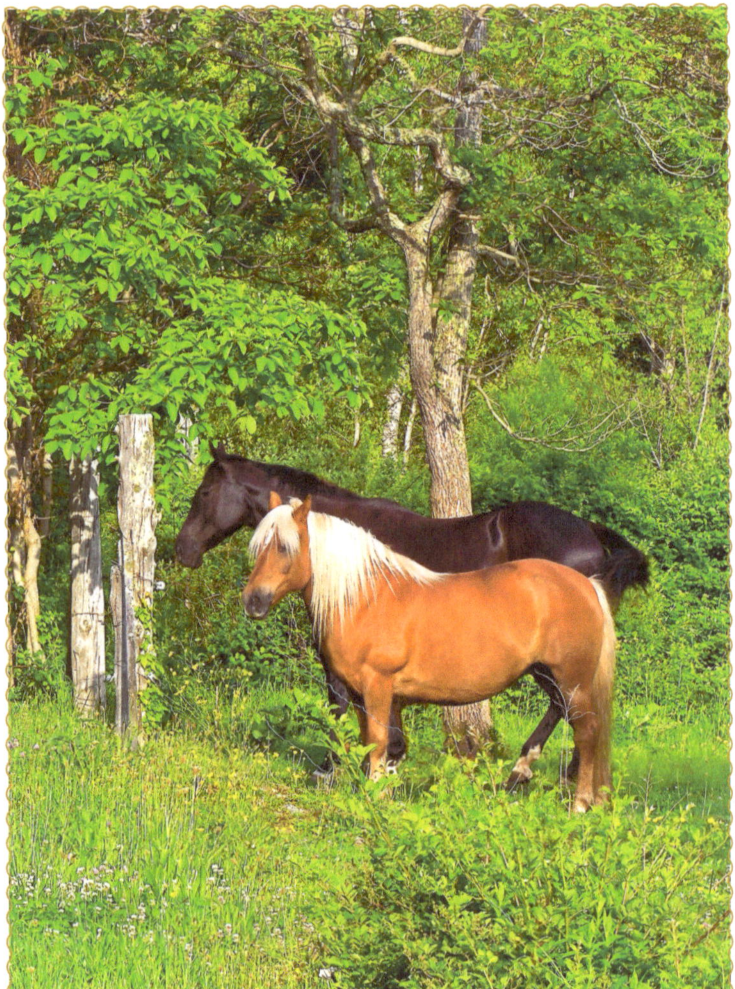

Wayne Gifford

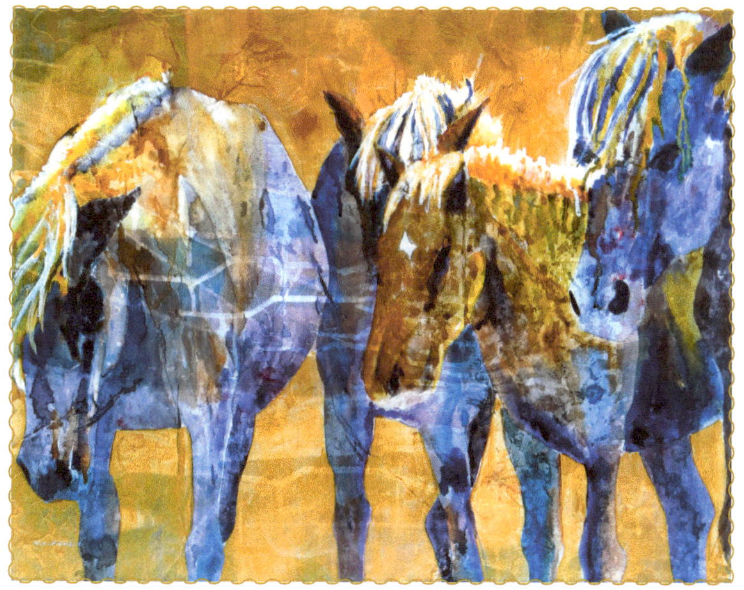

Meg MacKenzie

The one best precept—the golden rule in dealing with a horse—is never to approach him angrily. Anger is so devoid of forethought that it will often drive a man to do things which in a calmer mood he will regret.

Xenophon, (430 B.C.-354 B.C.)

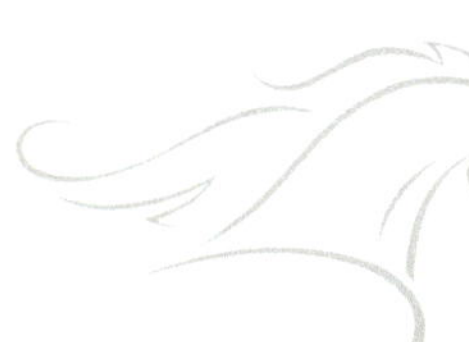

What does it take to train a horse? More time than the horse has.

Larry Mahan, (b. 1942)

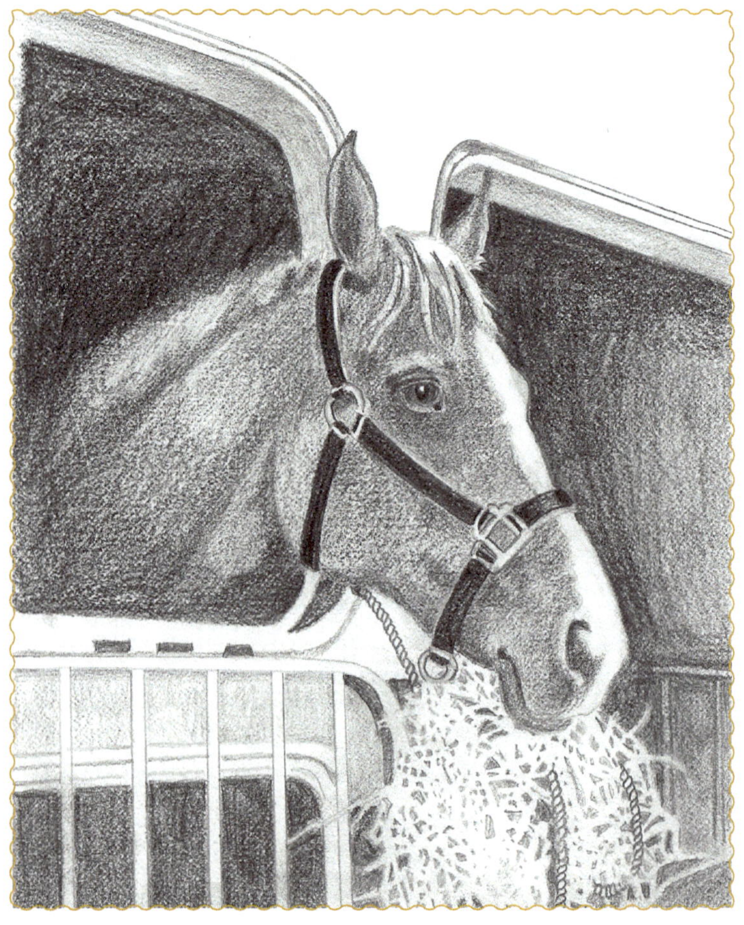

Jeanette Robertson

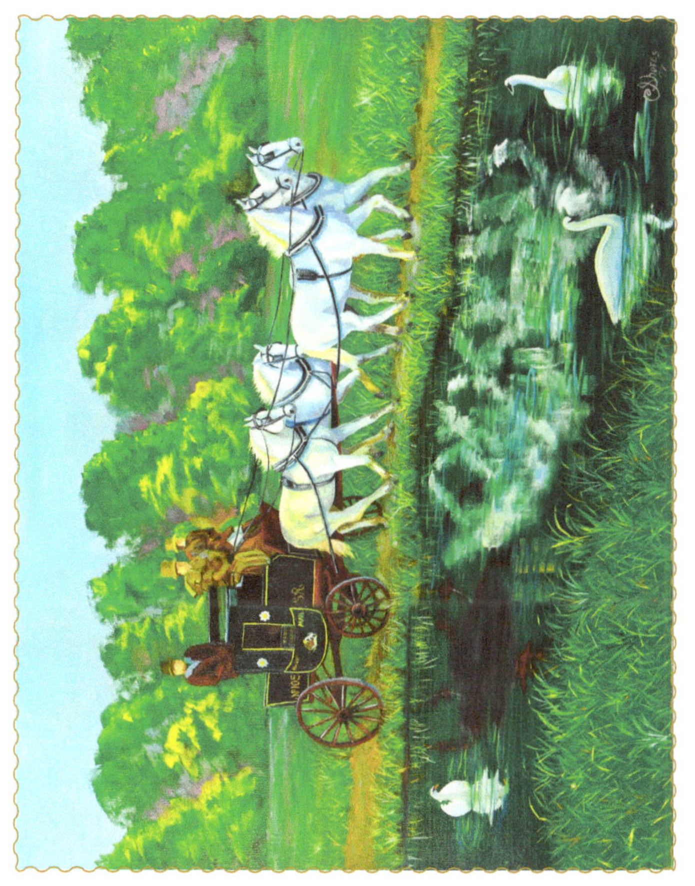

Charlotte Blanchard

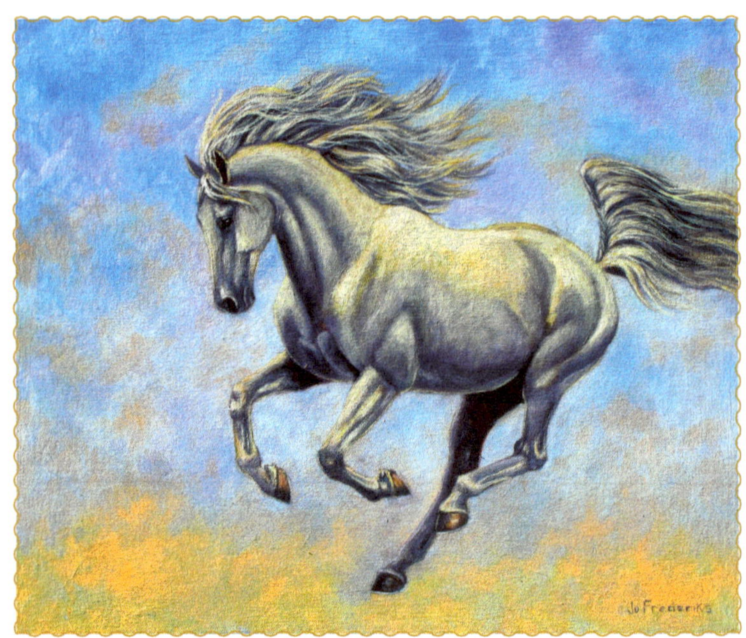

Jo Frederiks

Young hot colts being raged do rage the more.

William Shakespeare, (1564-1616)

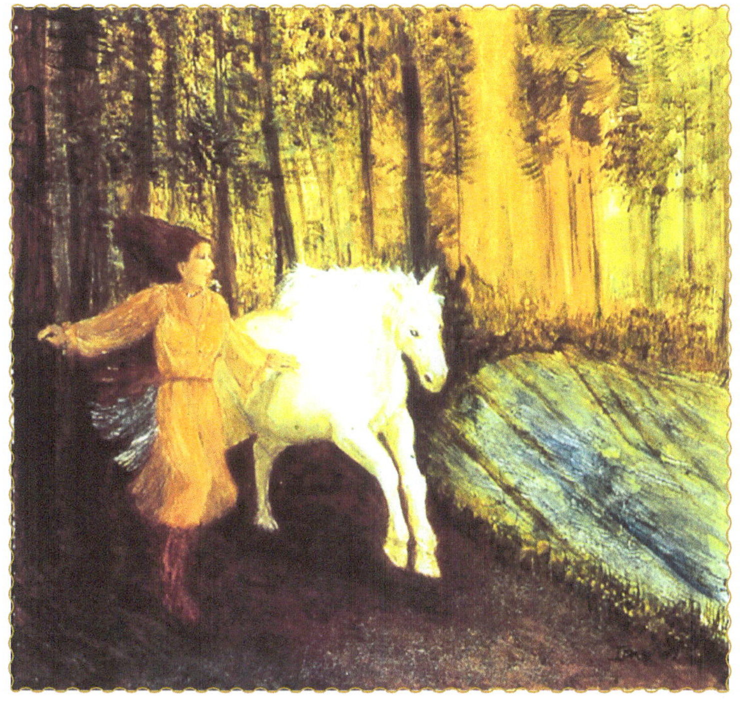

Ione Citrin

We shall take great care not to annoy the horse and spoil his friendly charm, for it is like the scent of a blossom—once lost it will never return.

Antoine de Pluvinel, (1552-1620)

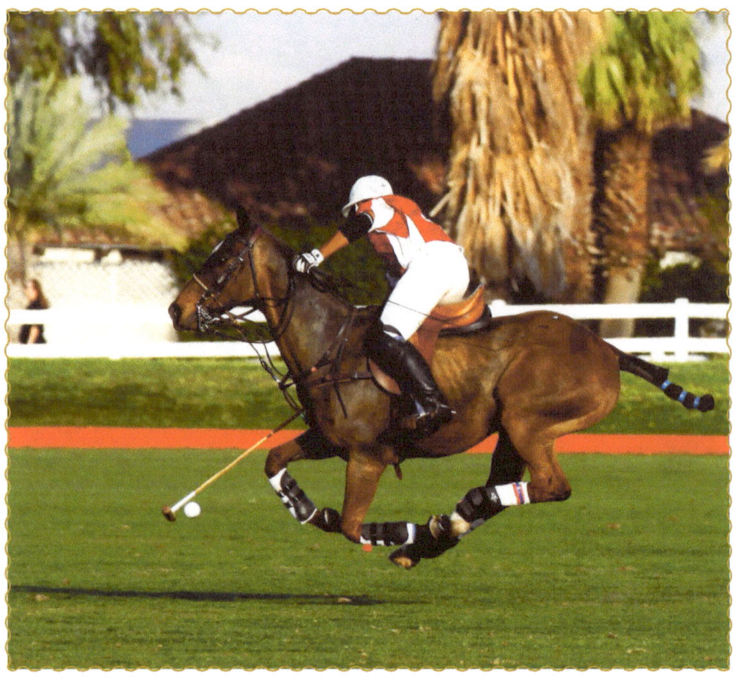

Romain Brumby

A horse doesn't care how much you know until he knows how much you care.

Pat Parelli, (b. 1955)

You cannot train a horse with shouts and expect it to obey a whisper.

Dagobert D. Runes, (1902-1982)

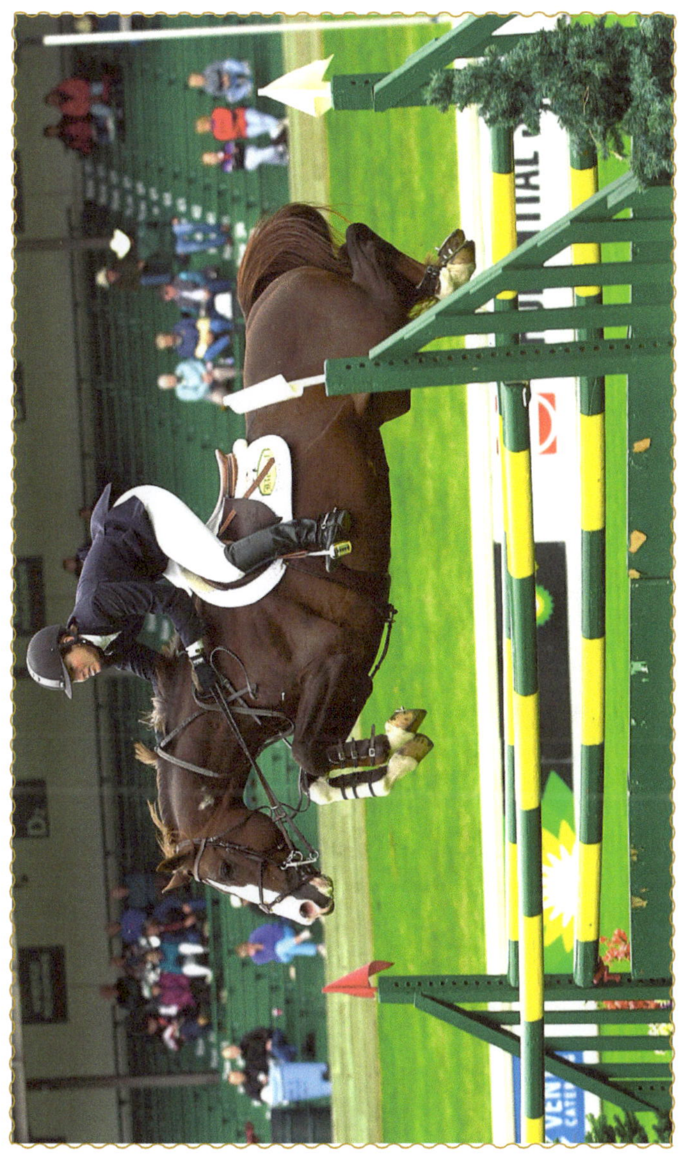

Beezie Madden by Peter Llewelly

For what the horse does under compulsion, as Simon also observes, is done without understanding, and there is no beauty in it either, any more than if one should whip and spur a dancer.

Xenophon, (430 B.C.-354 B.C.)

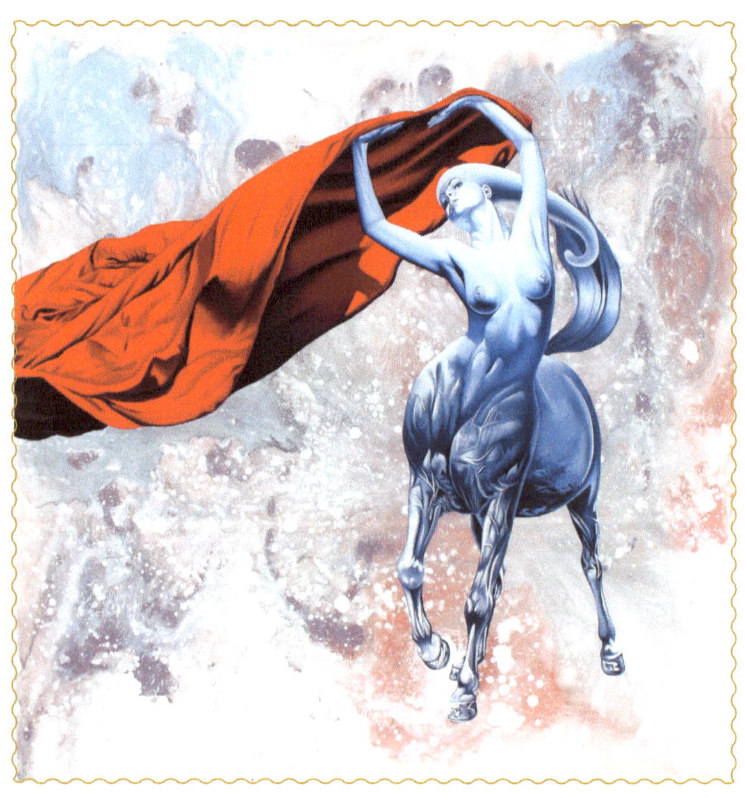

Graeme Stevenson

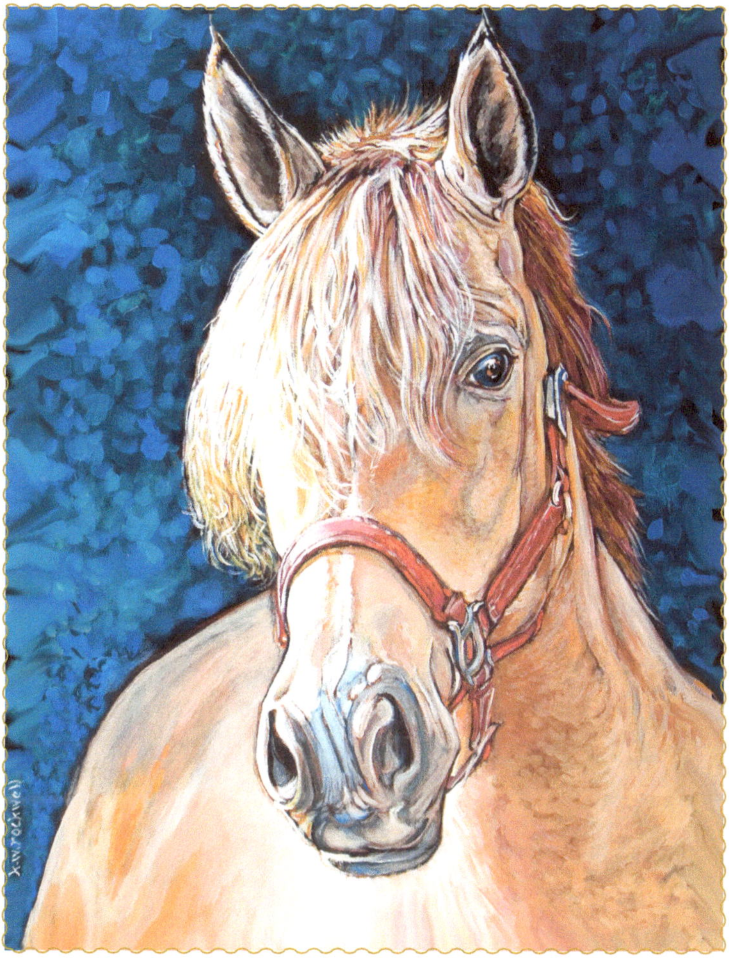

Kevin Rockwell

No one can teach riding so well as a horse.

C. S. Lewis, (1898-1963)

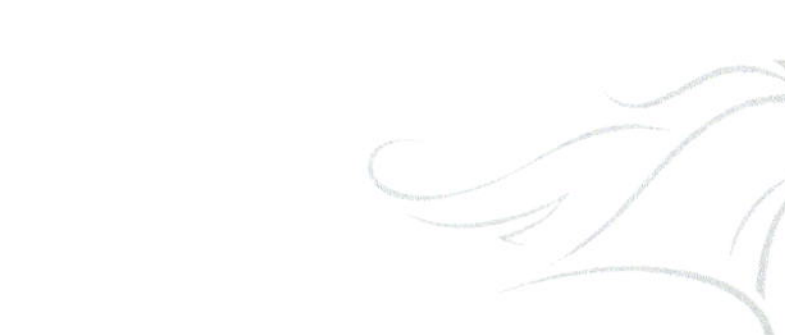

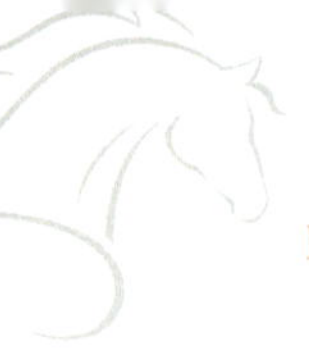

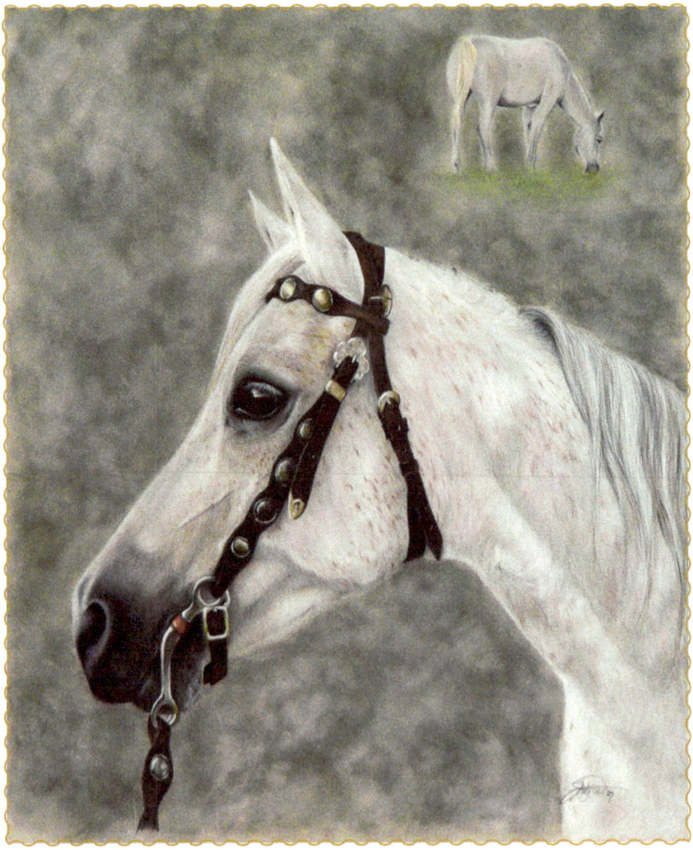

Jody Mateo

If you act like you've only got fifteen minutes, it'll take all day. Act like you've got all day and it'll take fifteen minutes.

Monty Roberts, (b. 1935)

There are many types of bits for many disciplines, but the severity of all bits lies in the hands holding them.

Monty Roberts, (b. 1935)

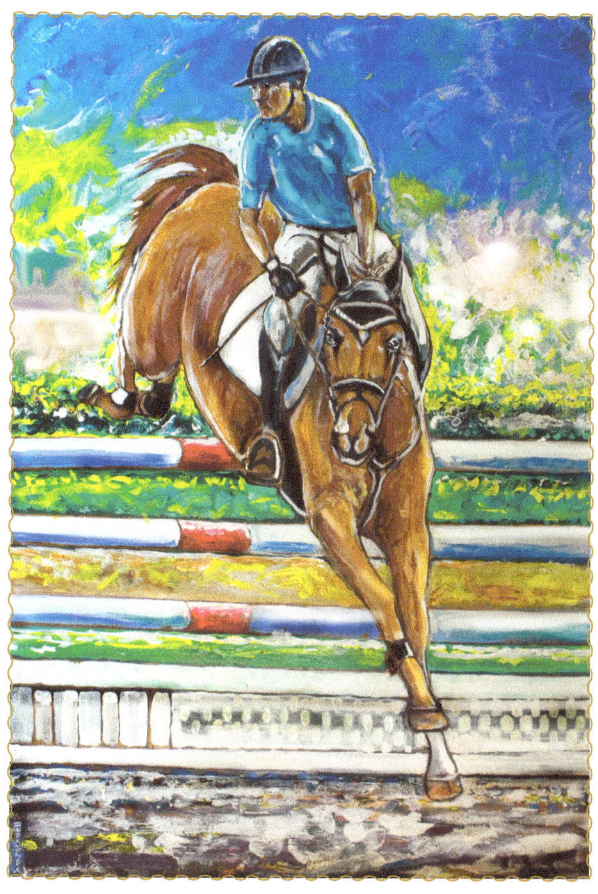

Kevin Rockwell

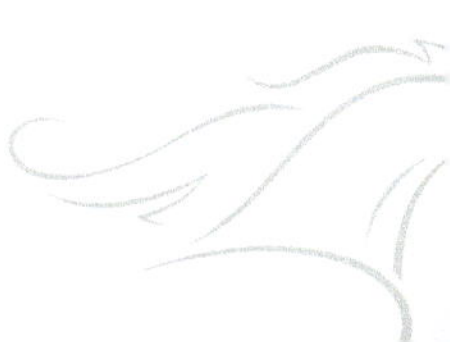

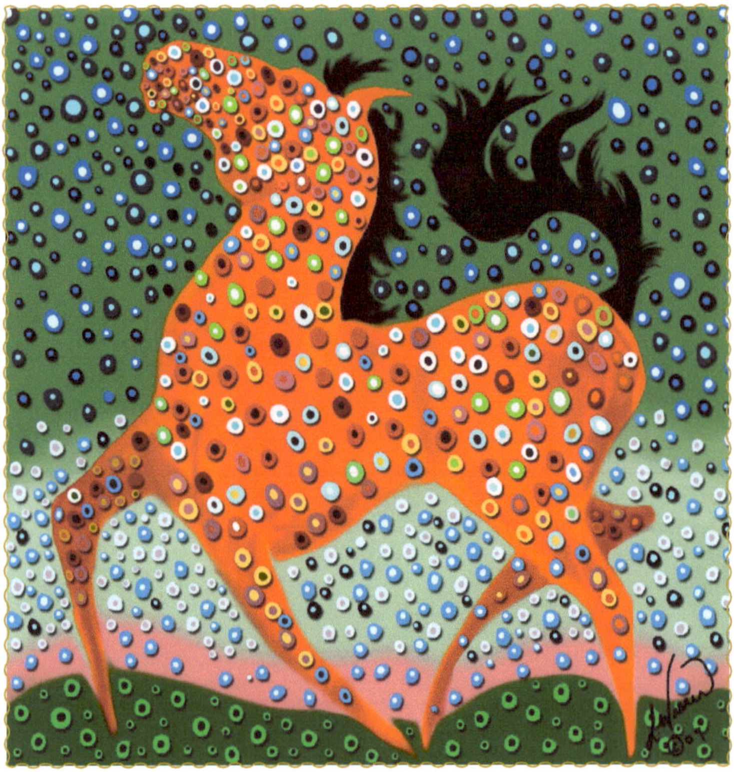

Lyndey Warren

We dominate a horse by mind over matter. We could never do it by brute strength.

Monica Dickens, (1915-1992)

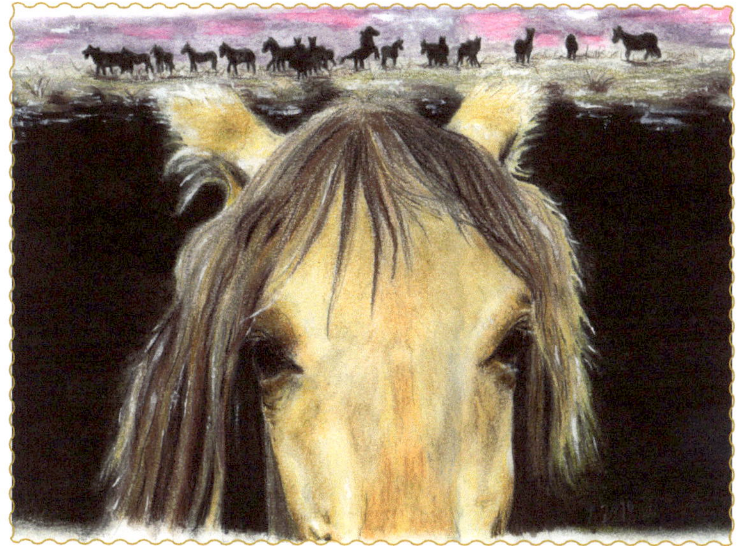

Yvonne Lautenschlager

Riders who force their horses by the use of the whip only increase their fear for they then associate the pain with the thing that frightens them.

Xenophon, (430 B.C.-354 B.C.)

A good cowboy will make whatever he's riding better—and a poor cowboy will be afoot even on a good horse.

Ray Hunt, (1929-2009)

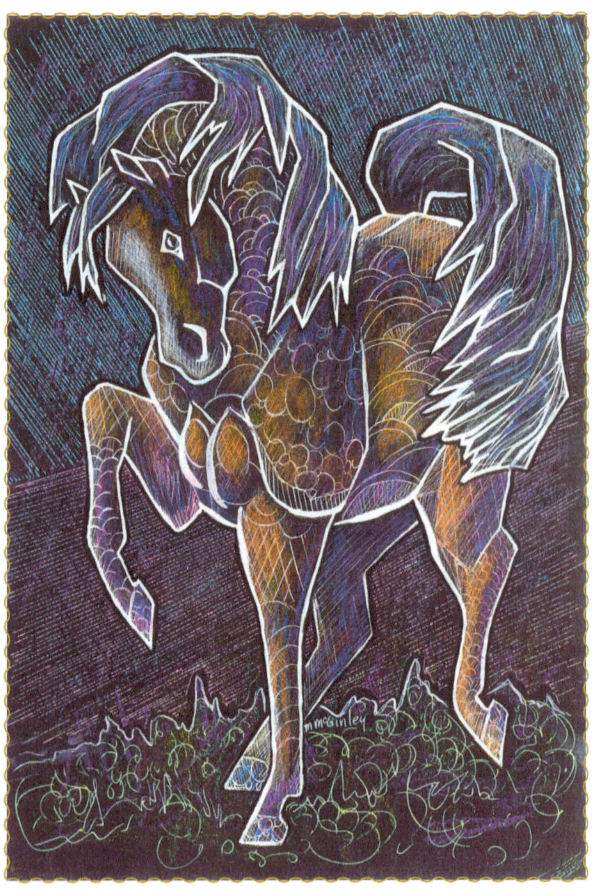

Marge McGinley

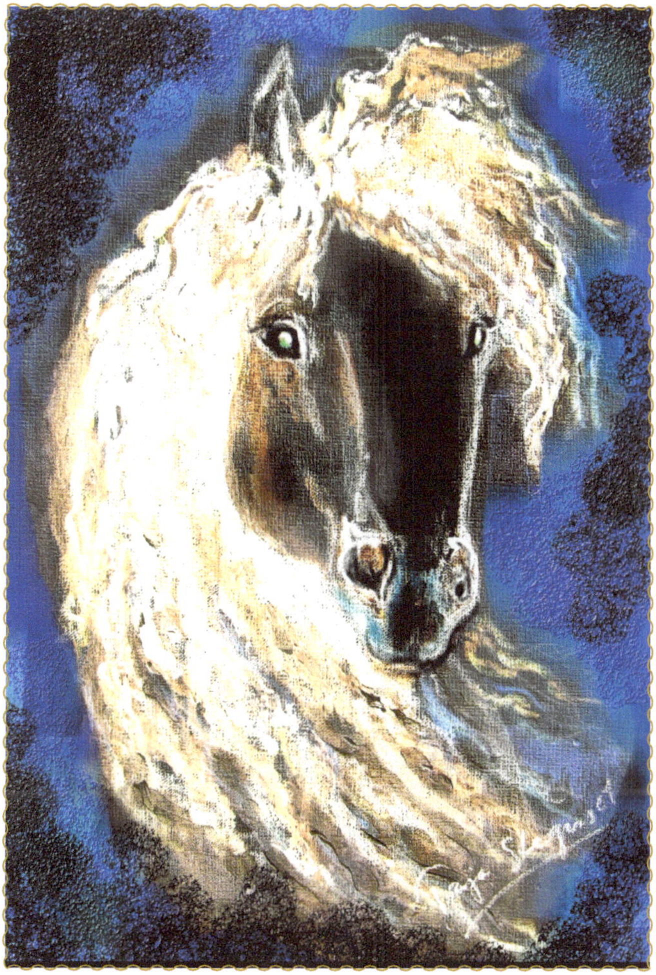

Tarja Stegars

In training horses, one trains himself.

Antonine De Pluvine, (1552-1620)

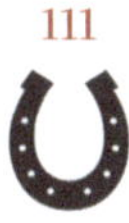

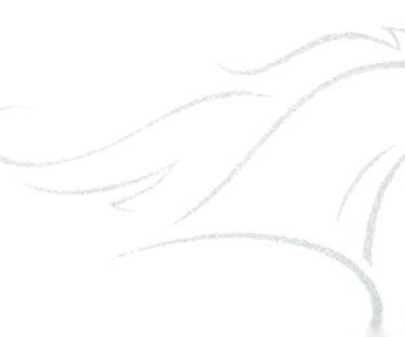

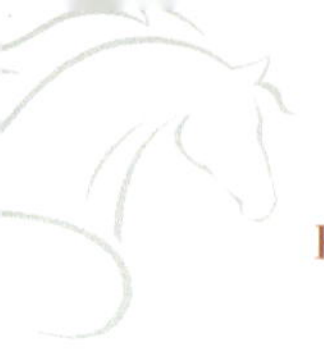

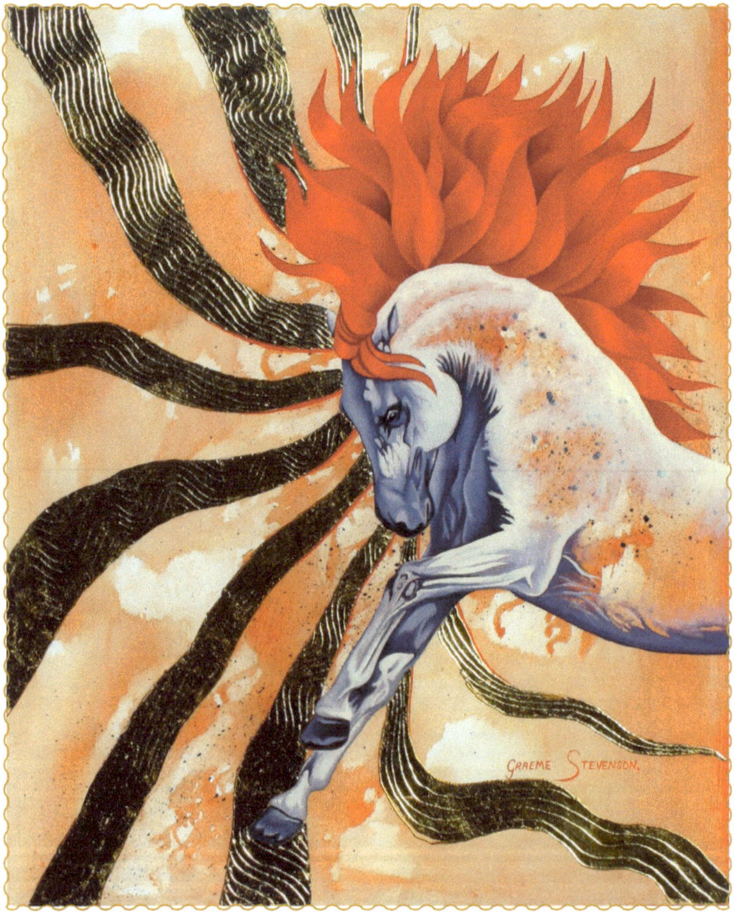

Graeme Stevenson

There is nothing in which a horse's power is better revealed than in a neat, clean stop.

Michel de Montaigne, (1533-1592)

There are only two emotions that belong in the saddle, one is a sense of humor and the other is patience.

John Lyons, (b. 19 ??)

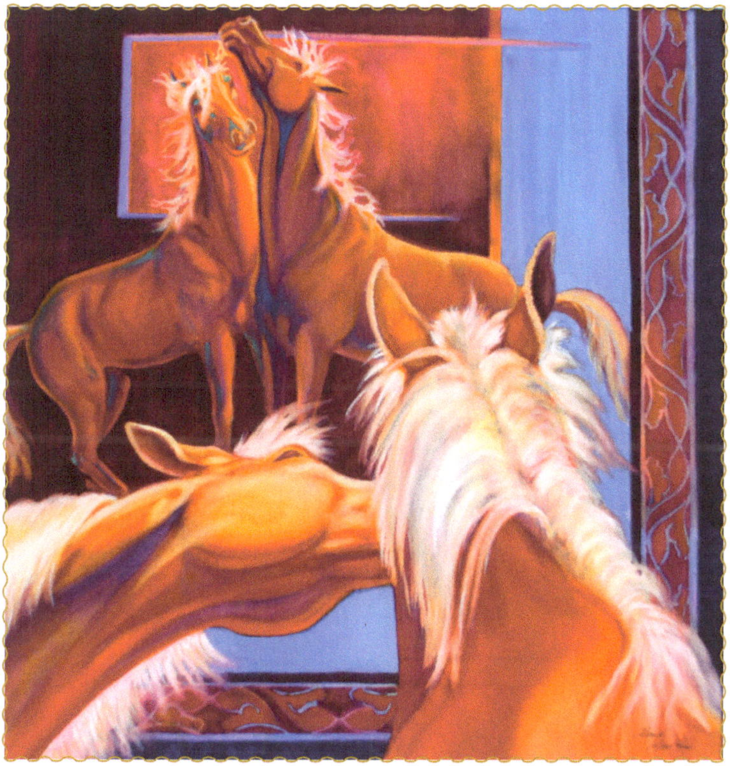

Robyn Ryan

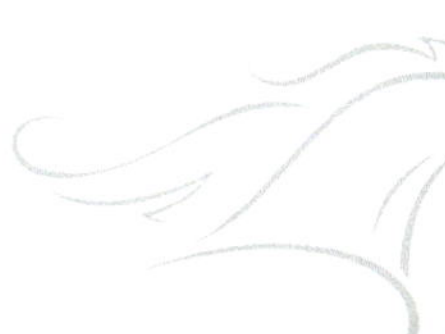

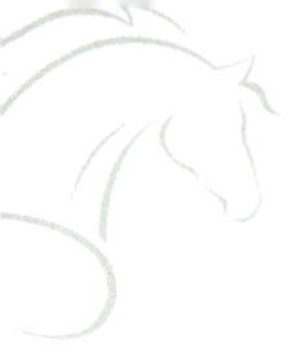

Artists & Photographers Biographies

Marika Anderson—Page 72

Marika works in a realistic, representational style and paint a variety of subjects, including landscapes, animals, plants, and boats, but horses are my favorite. Marika has a Bachelor's degree in Animal Science. Her formal art training is from numerous classes and workshops. She has shown her watercolor paintings throughout California and have won several awards. She participates annually in the Silicon Valley Open Studios and in the Santa Clara Valley Watercolor Society shows. See more of her artwork at **www.marikaart.com**

Charles Andrews III—Page 46

Charles Andrews III is a multifaceted artist who exhibits in many outdoor setting. His large paint on wood sculptures are known for the social and political statements they make. The controversial nature and location of some of his exhibits has caused local authorities to become involved.

Charles's studio, located south of Cazenovia, NY in Pig City, is open to visitor by appointment. For commission work contact him through facebook or by phone at 315 727 5370. The photo is of his Grandfather, the Honorable Judge Charles Andrews, making his rounds on horseback.

Faith Bailey—Page 40

Faith lives in County Wicklow in the Republic of Ireland, she came from Warwickshire in England originally. She is a part time artist, and a full time archaeologist. She does not have any formal art training but loves drawing. Pencil is her favorite medium however, she paints as well. When not drawing or working she spends time with her horse (Filly) and her two dogs (Oscar and Polly). Horses have always been her first love. See more of Faith's work or contact her about commission work at her website **www.faithbaileyart.co.uk** or on her facebook page Faith Bailey Equestrian Artwork.

Kerry Ball—Page 31, 43

Based in the Nottinghamshire region of the United Kingdom, Kerry Ball specializes in animal portraits and is also an amateur photographer. In 2009, Ball began her own photography business, Digital Country. Ball is also deeply involved in equestrian events and her work has been featured in All Horses Magazine, Equestrian Life Magazine and Nottinghamshire Today. Work can be viewed and purchased online at **www.digitalcountry.webs.com**.

Sergio Bartolacelli—Page 30

Sergio Bartolacelli was born on July 13, 1954 in the Modena Appenines. He now lives and works in Boccadiganda, a tiny hamlet of Borgoforte, near the Po River in the Province of Mantua in Lombardy, Italy. He has been drawing and painting from instinct since he was a boy, gifted with a hand that transfers to canvas or paper, that which his eyes see. His use of a monochromatic technique allows him to concentrate on the lines of the subject, which results in the work becoming more immediate, full of emotion, and very deeply striking.

Dana Bauer—Page 23, 25

Dana Bauer rode through her girlhood on club-hooved, cribbing, chestnut gelding called Apollo. From her years of laughter, heartbreak and glory with this complicated Morgan, Dana created Dana's Doodles. Her work has been published in Horse Illustrated, Young Rider, and Dressage Today. Her products are sold through Wild Horsefeathers, Bit of Britain, and online at **www.danasdoodles.com**

Charlotte Blanchard—Page 51, 65, 99

Growing up on a small family farm in Hubbardsville, New York, Charlotte can't remember not drawing or painting. As an only child, she

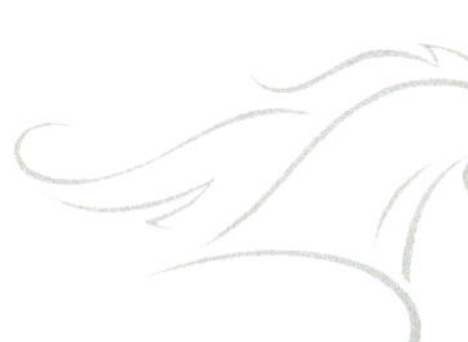

entertained herself for hours on end, escaping into the world of art. At the age of 11, the family made a drastic move to Florida, where Charlotte continued to find solace in the art world. Many of her paintings portray her love for horses and Upstate New York scenery. In 2008, Charlotte became overcome with artistic inspiration when she traveled to Italy for the first time. Her love for Italian architecture, the opulent Mediterranean Sea and the quaint villages came to life on her extraordinary oil canvases. Contact Charlotte at: Wishful Traveler Gallery Hubbardsville, New York 13355 T: 315-691-2265

E: **wishfultravelergallery@yahoo.com**
www.wishfultravelergallery.com

Romain Brumby—Page 73, 102

Romain is 19 years old in his second semester as a photography major student at Palomar College. He started photography a few years back when he bought my first reflex and got more and more interested and decided to study photography after high school. He lives in murrieta, CA and take pictures of the places he happen to be.

Contact Romain at **rrrooommmaaaiiinnn@gmail.com**

Tim Campbell—Page 36

Tim Campbell describes himself as a self-taught/outsider artist. His work can be seen in galleries throughout New England, Cape Cod, Atlanta and San Francisco. Additionally, his art is featured at the American Folk Art Gallery in New York City. His sculptural pieces are created entirely from recycled wood and metal. His painted furniture uses vintage pieces, which gives them their primitive appearance. Each piece is unique and one-of-a-kind. More information about Tim Campbell's work can be found at **www.tcampbellart.com** or on his facebook page Tim Campbell Art.

Laurence Cassin—Page 48

Laurence was born on April 1, 1973 and is a female model horse artist. She discovered her first model horses in Germany in 1987, and then started collecting, customizing, painting and making model tack for them. This is only a hobby and her main job is chiropodist. She started to sell her model tack pieces worldwide in 2005. She lives in Normandy, France.

People can see various examples of her miniature work on **http://www.haras-de-falde.com** or on her Facebook page "Laurence Haras de Falde"

Jackie Cercek—Page 80

Jackie lives in the high desert of southeastern Oregon. She is an amateur photographer and a retired psychologist and a retired college administrator. She started taking photos in 1957 when her dad gave her a Brownie camera. She loves the West and loves to shoot photos of typical western lore such as horses, cows, buckaroos, local ranch brandings, rodeos, western landscapes and desert scenery. In particular, she loves to photograph horses.

See more of her beautiful work at **www.jmathisenphoto.com**.

Cholla Chambers—Page 58, 60, 61

Cholla Chambers is an international artist. He has won 2 honorable mention Art Awards, one from Venice, Italy where he was also given a solo show in 2009. His art has shown in galleries across the USA including NYC, Vegas, Reno, & San Francisco. His art has been described as having "the fire of Pollock" and "the fixed gaze of Resnick". Yes he is a horse.

See Chapter 5 page 59 for more and you can learn more about Cholla and his art at **www.ArtistIsaHorse.com**

Ione Citrin—Page 12, 88, 101

Ione's art has shown nationally since 1998 when, after years of world travel, a successful television, radio, theatre and film career in the performing arts, she decided to focus her richly diverse talents on the visual arts. Ione's artistic expression, creativity, and passion for communication have resulted in numerous awards for her painting, sculpture, mixed media, and assemblage. Her work has also been featured in several important publications. Ione maintains an extensive exhibition schedule

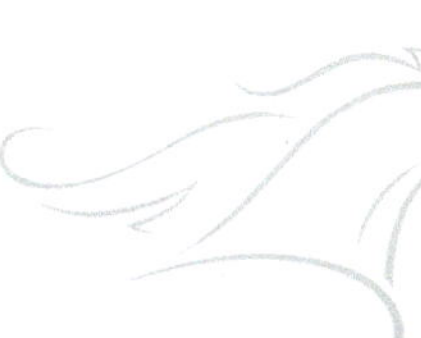

in juried, non-juried, and invitational arts venues. Contact her at Ione Citrin 2222 Avenue of the Stars, Suite 2302 Los Angeles CA 90067 phone: (310) 556-4382 **www.artbyione.com ICitrin@aol.com**

Kayla Clark—Page 49

Kayla is an artist and art teacher. She likes to work in reds and oranges as well as blue. Kayla is a member of the CNY Art Guild of America and has had many pieces of design and artwork published. She is available to teach art classes to students off all ages in painting, drawing, or sculpture from her studio in East Syracuse NY. Her website is **www.kaylaclarkart.com**. She can be reached at 315 415 2576 or **kaylaclarkart@hotmail.com**.

Joanne Elrod—Page 21, 24

Joanne Elrod started her artwork business, Tarimoor Art, in 2009, and has built it up into a recognizable brand with a reputation for providing quality art work and products. Although based in Yorkshire, in England, Joanne carries out commission work, and posts her art and products all over the world. The main focus of Joanne's work is working animals, and she has become known for her portrayal of them and the ability to capture the character of her subjects in a variety of media. She has also captured the humorous side of some of her subjects with a number of caricatures featuring dogs, horses and cats, some of which help raise funds for charity. You can see more of her work, and the products offered at **www.tarimoorart.co.uk**.

Sabrina Epifani—Page 82

Sabrina lives and works in Zurich Switzerland. Most of her training has been in Switzerland. She paints primarily in oil and acrylic on canvas. Sabrina fantasy art is characterized by vibrant colors and wonderful detail. She has exhibited extensively in Switzerland. View more of her wonderful art at **www.epifani.ch** or at her facebook page Sabrina Epifani.

Jo Frederiks—Page 8, 91, 100

Jo Frederiks was raised on a pristine million acre cattle station in remote central Queensland. This environment nurtured her love and spiritual connection to horses, animals and natures magic, which still influences her today. She has been a passionate vegan, and animal rights activist for much of her life. All of this has culminated in her choice to become an Equine and Animal Artist. Jo's education was formal study at the Arts Academy in Brisbane had her achieve Honors in Professional Studies, Advanced Studio practice and fine Art and Illustration. Jo works with oils and various drawing media and renders in an Impressionistic Style. Her objective is to create, beauty, grace, strength and sensitivity of the magnificent's, that is the horse. Jo's foremost passion is to raise awareness of animal suffering. See her work at **www.jofrederiks.com**.

Wayne G. Gifford—Page 96

Wayne Gifford lives in Fairhaven Massachusetts, a quaint seaside community that looks over Buzzards Bay, Cape Cod and the Islands. His inspirations come from an accessibility of diverse local venues ranging from seascapes, wildlife, sunsets and sunrises, seasonal and horticulture. His photography is currently available to view at Blue Collar Photography on facebook or by contacting him through facebook.

Gene Gissin—Page 64

Gene Gissin is a graduate of RIT College of Graphic Arts and Photography. He owns Gene Gissin Photography where he specializes in photographing everything from weddings to pets. Further, Gissin also works in photojournalism and has taught photography at Cazenovia College in Cazenovia, New York. Today, he is the President of the Professional Photographers Society of Central New York. For more of Gissin's work, visit his website at **www.gissinphoto.com**

Judy Goldthwait—Page 38, 55

Judy graduated from Cazenovia College in 1998, with a BFA in Commercial Illustration. Ever since, she has been a respected artist in the equine field. By specializing in equine art and pet portraiture, Judy

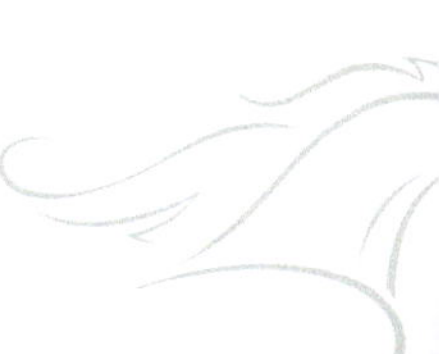

has found a way to make a living by painting what she knows best. Inspiration for her paintings often derives from photos she has taken at horse shows or other events. However, most of her work is done for private commission. Judy has illustrated posters and designed promotional material for the Intercollegiate Horse Show Nationals, the Intercollegiate Dressage Association Nationals, the New England Quarter Horse Association, the New England Equitation Championships, as well as the Lorenzo Driving Competition. Her paintings have been exhibited all over the country, most recently in the Master of Foxhounds Association Centennial Traveling Art Exhibition. Clients are numerous and span the United States as well as Canada, England, Holland and France. See more of her work at **www.jgpetportraits.com**.

Kyleen Hafferkamp—Page 45

Kyleen has had a passion for photography starting at a young age. The passion grew when she moved to Northern Colorado and she couldn't help but capture the scenes around her. She finds beauty in things she sees everyday, but those in urban areas may not. Horses, cattle, fences, ranching equipment, etc. She tries to bring those people into her life through her photographs. By conveying the feelings of the animals or person she is photographing, she hopes to tell a story, different for each person looking at the photograph. See her work at **www.khimaging.com** or on facebook at KH Imaging Photography

Polly Holabird—Page 18, 34, 53

Polly, a true horse lover, has been drawing, riding, painting, showing, cartooning, training, and just hanging around horses all her life. Her delightful artwork is available in a variety of forms from posters, to T-shirts, to jean jackets, and more. Polly runs her art business from a small farm way out in the woodsy mountains of Massachusetts. She sells wholesale and retail. She also travels to major horse shows and fairs throughout the USA displaying her work.

View all her artwork at **www.pollypaintbrush.com**.

Richard Ledyard Hubbard (1903-1993)—Page 68, 90

Mr. Hubbard studied art with Cazenovia artist, Dwight Williams before beginning his formal training at the Pennsylvania Academy of Fine Arts. He exhibited bronzes at the National Academy in New York and at his alma mater in Philadelphia. He had a one-man show at the Montrose Gallery in New York City and received first prize at the Boston Festival of Art in 1955.

The painting on page 68 is owned by Georgeann Redmond and the painting on page 90 is owned by Polly Koerner.

Kary Kidder—Page 87

Kary Kidder is a passionate horse and dog lover from Covington, Washington. She is the caregiver of no less than six pugs, three of which are rescue dogs. Kidder has quite literally raised a small zoo of animals, ranging from chickens and rabbits to hermit crabs, donkeys, snakes and lizards. She is also the owner of www.onesmugpug.com, a site dedicated to commission portraits of pet portraits. Kary also sells her art at **www.zazzle.com/karykid**. Recently, Kidder has won several awards for her oil paintings and is now working in photography.

Susan Kordish—Page 83

Susan has been a photographer for a number of years. She has done freelance work for "The Horse", and "Trail Blazer" magazine. She has had work appear in Yankee Pedlar and a Canadian Team Penning magazine. She is a member of the Association of Photoshop Professionals and the Professional Photographers Association. She has taken some college level classes, online classes and just attended an amazing Photoshop seminar. Susan has recently begun entering photography contest and some juried art shows. She also makes and sells photo note cards. Visit her website **www.azcowgirlphotography.com** her facebook page Cowgirl Photography or contact her at Susan Kordish PO Box 204 Skull Valley, Arizona 86338 **cowgirlphotography@hughes.net**

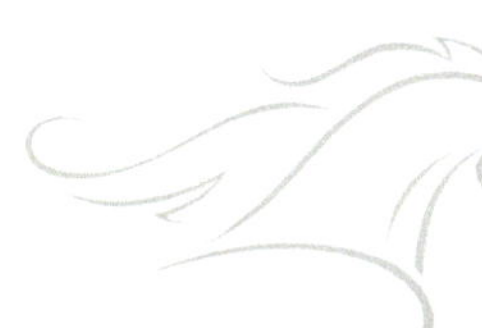

Christian Lathom-Sharp—Page 89

Christian is a freelance photographer based in Bristol in the South West of England. She was lucky enough to be given her first camera when she was about 9, it was a bright red Kodak point and shoot. Both her Grandpa and Dad were keen photographers so naturally she caught the bug and it's stuck with her ever since. In her teens she stumbled upon art college and years of study, painting and drawing have further given her a strong eye for composition and the confidence to know what makes for a great shot. You can contact Christian or see more of her work at:

www.facebook.com/horseandriderphoto
www.horseandriderphotography.co.uk
Tel: 07897 396639 43 Romney Ave, Lockleaze Bristol BS7 9ST

Yvonne Lautenschlager—Page 109

Yvonne Lautenschlager is a Hamburg, Germany based artist. She has a medical degree and has worked in Orthopedic Medicine as well as Chinese Medicine. She is married with an eighteen-year-old son, a dog and two cats. Yvonne is very active creating new art, writing and maintaining her blog.

To see more of Yvonne's work, visit **medeasspace.blogspot.com**.

Sian Lewis—page 81

Sian Lewis is a freelance equestrian photographer from Cardiff, Wales, who specializes in horse and pony portraits. Sian has been a horse lover her whole life, which she attributes to her mum and aunty and so photographing these beautiful animals really is a dream job. Sian feels that her knowledge and understanding of horses and ponies allows her to capture their true spirit, thus producing beautiful portraits that show the horse as its very best. Though she is based in Wales, Sian has been as far a field as Kentucky to photograph horses.

www.equineimaging.co.uk
equineimaging@gmail.com
+44 7067 205474

Meg MacKenzie—Page 50, 97

Meg MacKenzie an award winning and acclaimed artist has her work in both international and national private collections. She draws her inspiration from the complex color formed by the early morning and late afternoon sunlight. The acrylic pieces reflect nature's patterns with texture, moodiness and unexpected color. She is a member of the Potomac Valley Watercolorists, Baltimore watercolor Society, Virginia Watercolor Society, The Art League in Old Town Alexandria, the Arlington Artists Alliance and the Northern Virginia Watercolor Workshop. She has shown in the Tidewater Virginia area, has done commissioned work and murals in the Shenandoah Valley, and now lives and shows in Northern Virginia. Her website is **www.megmackenzieart.com** and her telephone number is703 524 4482.

Elizabeth (Beezie) Madden—Page 62, 103

Beezie is an American Show jumping competitor and Olympic gold medal winner from Cazenovia, New York. She is trained by her husband, John Madden, who also runs his business, John Madden Sales, from their farm in Cazenovia. Two of her most popular horses are, Authentic (p.62) and Judgement. At the 2004 Summer Olympics in Athens, Beezie won the gold medal as part of the United States team in team jumping. At the 2008 Beijing Summer Olympics she earned a second gold in the team jumping competition. She also earned a bronze in the Individual Show Jumping competition. In 2008 Beezie placed first in the Animal Planet Sport Horse cup aboard Judgement. In 2004 Beezie was the first woman ever to pass the $1 million mark in show jumping earnings, a record she still holds. The photo on page 103 is by Peter Llewelly.

Melissa Mason—Page 84

Melissa currently resides in central Florida. Her artwork is part of the permanent collection of the Museum of Florida Art (Deland) and the Museum of Art & Science (Daytona Beach). Melissa's work has also appeared in numerous magazines and won several awards. Her website is **www.melissamason.org**.

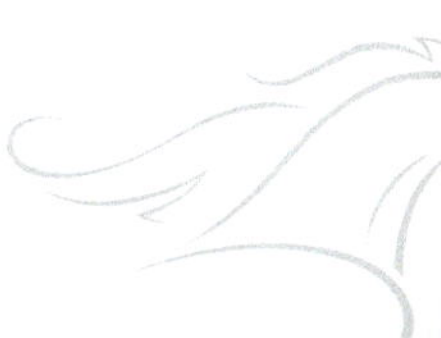

Jody Mateo—Page 106

Jody is a self taught artist. She has had an interest in art and a talent for drawing all her life. She began creating pet portraits in late 2003. Pastel on suede is the painting method she loves. It allows her pet portraits to pop with realism.

See her beautiful work at **www.portraityourpet.com**.

Emily Mayman—Page 32

Emily is a traditional equine artist from the UK. Emily's award winning equestrian artwork portrays her passion in its exceptional accuracy and detail, which she believes artists need to have, to create portraits people will treasure for a lifetime. She prides herself in the number of satisfied customers who are thrilled that their horse portraits capture their individual 'spark' and character - something that is hard to capture in two dimensional artwork, especially of the renowned challenging equine form. Visit her website at **www.theequineartist.co.uk** for more on her artwork.

Marge McGinley—Page 86, 110

Marge feels more alive when in the presence of a horse. Growing up on a North Dakota farm put her in touch with the "work team", a collection of big, strong steeds, and often riding bareback. When not astride a horse, she would be drawing them. When she graduated from high school she went to college with the dream of becoming an art teacher. Her style allows her to express the energy of the horse with color, pattern, and detail that is representative of the horse but not close photo-realism. She prefers to let her imagination guide her through each piece of art she creates. Contact Marge about her artwork at **marge@horsesofcourse.ws**. Or visit her website **www.horsesofcourse.ws**.

Gilda Meyers—page 20

The theme of Gilda's work reflects the abundant regional wildlife and equestrian traditions of the Arkansas, Texas and Oklahoma area. She chooses to depict wildlife and horses in there normal activities i.e. a solitary black bear roaming in the woods, majestic horses grazing in piney wood pastures or racing across a rocky river.As an artist, she hopes to stir a memory in those who see her work. To have them see the strength and beauty in wild and domestic animals. She won honors at numerous art awards.

Her artwork can be seen at www.southwestartists.org—select Gilda Meyers and www.ouachitaarttrails.com—select Gilda Meyers

Dee Dee Murry—Page 41, 56

Dee Dee Murry was born and raised in the Pacific Northwest. Her main interests in art subjects are horses, dogs and wildlife. She has achieved many regional and national awards with her art, including being the Washington State Ducks Unlimited Artist of the Year, 1st place in the Wildlife division in 'The Artist's' magazine, and reaching the top 10 in the highly competitive Federal Duck Stamp competition several times. Her love for animals shows through in her art where she strives to capture the personality and essence of the individual animal, as well as close attention to correct anatomy and detail.

Visit her website at www.deedeemurry.com.

Diane Nicholls—Page 17

Diane paints with fun and color in mind. Life should be fun, full of energy and joy. Most of her paintings have some type of message in them, but some are just for fun. Absence of detail is an objective she uses in her style of painting. Fauvism is probably closest to her style. See the favorite artists tab above to view some of the artists that have influenced her work.

Born in a suburb of Pittsburgh, attended college in Ohio (Landscape Architecture), raised 3 beautiful children and has now begun a new adventure in the Houston area. Her website is http://artdianenicholls.com

Joseph Palotas—Page 78

Joe Palotas is an experienced commission artist and works in many media. He infuses wild expressions of color to a wide variety of subject matter from portraits, to abstracts to contemporary and mixed media landscapes. His works reflect a variety of creative styles. See more of Joe's

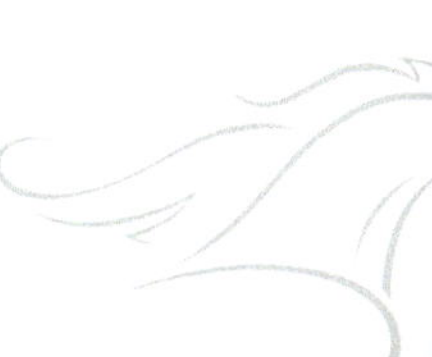

work at his facebook page Art In Wonderland or on his websites, **http://www.artsinwonderland.com**.

Kathryn Ragan—Page 44

Kathryn Ragan produces her paintings from a small farm outside of beautiful Vancouver, British Columbia. For the last ten years, Ragan, a self-taught artist, has worked in watercolor due to her love of the medium's "transparency, fluidity and unpredictability." Recently, Ragan was accepted into the International Guild of Realism. See more of her work at **www.studioatthefarm.ca**.

Georgeann "Gigi" Redmond—Page 69

Gigi riding Val over fences in about 1971. Painted in oil on canvas by Peter Irving.

Jeanette Robertson—Page 98

Jeanette is an artist and published author of art books [see them on amazon.com]. She works in watercolor and graphite pencil. Jeanette specializes in pet drawings but does much more.

You can find her art on: **www.CottageArtStudio.Etsy.com** or **www.jeanetterobertson.com** Contact her at **jrobertsonart@aol.com**

Kevin W. Rockwell—Page 6, 105, 107

Kevin W. Rockwell graduated from the Ringling College of Art and Design in 1980 with a focus in illustration and design. He has worked as a medical illustrator for the Medical University of South Carolina. Rockwell is currently active in different pet focused charitable organizations, such as the Pet Helpers pet shelter in Charleston, South Carolina. For the last ten years, Rockwell has been painting pets including dogs and horses. More than 70 paintings can be viewed online at his site **www.RockwellArts.com**.

Robyn Ryan—Page 13, 113

Robyn's paintings of landscapes and animals, wild or domestic, are a celebration of the wonder of God's creation. She has grown to appreciate each animal as an individual, with its own personality, behavior and perspective on the world. Her painting and sculptor also represent a mirror of ourselves, magnifying how we relate to the world and each other.

She can be contacted at Robyn Ryan P.O. Box 865, Fredericksburg, VA 22404 **rryan@hughes.net www.absolutearts.com/robynryan**

Carolyn Schlam—Page 15, 71

Carolyn Schlam is a painter, mixed media and glass artist living and working in Taos, New Mexico. She is also an illustrator of children's books and the author of "The Creative Path: Process and Practice". Her work can be seen on her website at www.carolynschlam.com and purchased directly or through the galleries that represent her work. Her work can be purchased also online through www.artquiver.com. Contact Carolyn through her website, her email at **carolynschlam@aol.com**, or by phone at 786-897-2276. She accepts commissions in all media.

Patricia Elliott Seitz—Page 14,

Patricia was born in San Diego California, and spent most of her young adulthood living in Southern California. She came from a background of art and music, and always knew that she wanted to be an artist. Her love for landscapes and seascapes has been heavily influenced by where she has lived through the years. Her painting approach is based on Impressionism, and Tonalism. Her main subject matter is landscapes, and seascapes. Today she can be found in her studio, painting seasonal paintings of the Central New York area, and the California coastlines. She is an active member of Oil Painters of America, CNY Art Guild, and her work is represented by Local NY art Galleries. See more of her work at **www.patriciaseitz.com**.

Carry Smith—Page 52

Carry comes from a very artistic and creative family background. She has drawn all her life and is proud to say she is a self-taught artist. She exhibits her work in competitions and art shows throughout Brisbane, the Gold Coast and the Sunshine Coast. Carry participated in several successful joint exhibitions. Her work is represented in private,

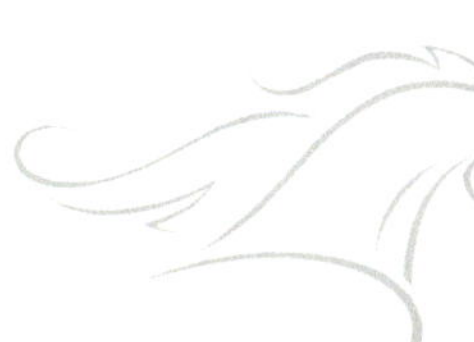

public and corporate collections throughout Brisbane, Melbourne, the Gold Coast, Sunshine Coast and the UK. View her work on her website www.carrysmith.com or on facebook under Carry Smith. Contact her by email at artist@carrysmith.com.

Tarja Stegars—Page 94, 111

Tarja Stegars is a plastic surgeon and artist living in Finland. She has had close contact with horses from childhood on. Horses are her friends, teachers and symbols of power, light and freedom. She shares her love for horses with her daughter Terhi Stegars, an accomplished dressage rider at the international grand prix level. Tarja was taught in her art by her father Rolf Stegars the renown chief scenic designer of the Finnish National Theater in Helsinki, Finland. Tarja wishes to portray the horse in her art as a subject in its own right without human restrictions such as saddles or other tack. See more of her wonderful artwork at www.egina.fi or on her facebook page Horse Art—Visions of Equines

Graeme Stevenson—Page 11, 79, 104, 112

Graeme Stevenson began painting and studying animals at five years old. His talent progressed rapidly and he began to explore the vast areas of Australia, photographing, sketching, and eventually painting the exotic animals of this land. Graeme then began traveling to other parts of the world to study his subjects and to display his work. Africa, India, Malaysia, Indonesia, Japan, Europe, U.K., U.S.A., Mexico, Canada, Alaska and the Middle East were some of the places to which he ventured, receiving offers from publishers who produced his works in limited edition. He has continued his artistic work with many well received art show and more recently art TV shows. Read more about Graeme's amazing career and see his wonderful artwork at www.graemestevenson.com.au or Graeme Stevenson on facebook.

Kristin Taylor—Page 74, 95

Kristin Taylor lives in Ithaca, NY where she works as a civil engineer and assists with coaching the Cornell University First Year and JV Polo teams. An avid polo player, Kristin played on the Cornell team in college and now owns her own polo ponies that she keeps at her farm. Her artwork consists of everything equine, in media including graphite, watercolor, oil, pastel, and glass etching. In 2008 she started an art business called Offside Art where she focuses on commissioned portraits of horses and pets. To see more of her artwork visit her website at www.offsideart.com.

Jeanne M. Thieme—Page 28, 76, 92

Jeanne's work embodies subject matter that she is passionate about—local rural landscapes, floral and animals-particularly horses. She has chosen to paint the experience of having horses in her life and their amazing energy rather than a realistic illustration of their bodies. Jeanne's bold brushwork helps her to capture a horse's movement and energy without focusing on minute details. Each of her paintings has a goal and an intent-it is her challenging and exciting task to find the tools, soul and bravery to make it happen! Jeanne believes so strongly in the power of the brushstroke that she does not produce prints of her work. Her customers receive a truly original piece to treasure. See more of her artwork on her website; www.jmthiemefinearts.com

Samantha Thompson—Page 42

Samantha Thompson's pastel and acrylic paintings display a complex of influences from her rich and varied life. She was born in Sydney in 1978. Having worked and exhibited around the world including New York and London, her last major influence was living in the most 'art deco' city in the universe, Napier in New Zealand. Samantha's paintings are a masterful blend of form, style and content, incorporating the rich habitat she has encountered during her short itinerant life. Visit her facebook page Samantha Thompson—Artist or view her artwork at www.samanthathompson.com.au

Hannah Tippett—Page 10, 67, 70

Hannah runs Tyack Photography a small photography company in Cornwall UK with Kathie Tippett. They mainly cover weddings and equestrian events but also have a range of other services including babies

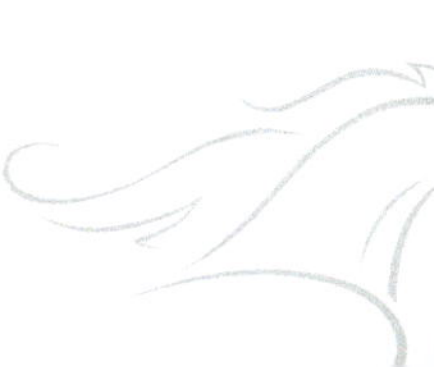

and boudoir. See more of Hannah's work at **www.tyackphotography.webs.com** or on facebook at Tyack Photography.

Karen Travis—Page 85

Karen Travis lives in Park City, Utah, where she is able to use the beauty of nature for inspiration. Travis has enjoyed a love of painting for as long as she can remember. She received her Masters in Illustration from Syracuse University in New York State. Travis draws heavily on her own life experiences for inspiration in creating her work. She hopes to allow others to feel part of the joy she has discovered within the creative process. More of her art can be viewed at **www.kaleidascopedesigns.com**

Pamela Utton—Page 27

Residing in Baker, Florida Pam Utton is a self-taught artist who has emerged her love of animals and art. In fact, it was her love of animals that inspired her to paint. Today, Utton is frequently called upon to paint pets from around the world. She is also an avid photographer and home designer. Her websites include **www.pamutton.blogspot.com** and two online stores **www.etsy.com/shop/petportraitart** and **www.zazzle.com/pamutton**. Visit her on facebook.

Erica Marie Veit—Page 26, 54, 75

Erica attended the Savannah College of Art and Design and competed with their equestrian team. She recently graduated from the College of Charleston with degrees in Studio Art and Arts Management. The quality of her equine, oil on canvas, paintings capture her personal experience and knowledge of multiple riding disciplines. Erica specializes in custom equine and canine portraits and she welcomes commissions. Contact her at **erica.marie.veit@gmail.com**. View more of her work at **www.ericamarieveit.wordpress.com**.

Lyndsey Warren—Page 47, 108

Lyndsey holds a BFA from the Hartford Art School with a focus on children's book and scientific illustration, as well as minors in photography and art history. She continued her education onward to obtain a

MAT/MFA from the Maryland Institute College of Art. Lyndsey has become a highly marketable artist and illustrator. She has worked on designs, illustrations, websites, and logos for equine related businesses, local vintners, musicians, video and online game producers, concepts for film and entertainment, veterinarians, and local schools. She has experience with working with graphic and website designers, art directors, and museum curators.

Visit her website at **www.shadowhorsestudios.com**

Julie Wheler—Page 33, 37

Julie is a horse and dog lover. Photography is one of her many hobbies. Horses and dogs are among her favorite subjects to photograph.

Leigh Willson—Page 9

Leigh is a photographer with Summerhill Farm in Mooi River, Kwazulu-Nasal, South Africa. Contact her about her work by email at **dejavu_c24@yahoo.co.uk**

Valarie Wolf—Page 22

Valarie Wolf is an artist who resides in Orange County, California where she lives with her husband and two energetic Italian Greyhounds. Wolf is also a member of the American Academy of Equine Art. Valarie is passionate about animals in general and donates part of the proceeds of her paintings to various animal welfare groups. Learn more about Valarie and her art at **www.valariewolf.com**

Rick Young—Page 16

Rick is a self-taught artist from St Louis. He works in many mediums including graphite, charcoal, oil, pastel, and encaustic (wax paint), which is now his main medium. His subjects are many, and usually no two paintings are similar. He currently is working on a series of encaustic paintings based on Revelations entitled "The Seven Seals". Visit his website at **www.encaustichorse.com**

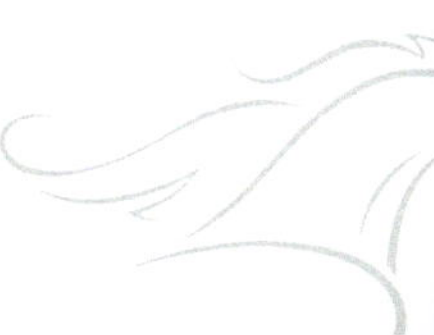

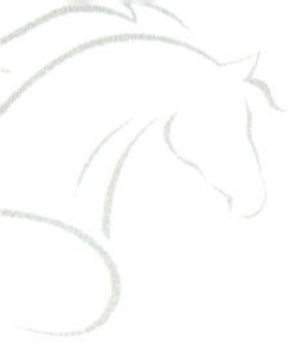

Index of Quotations

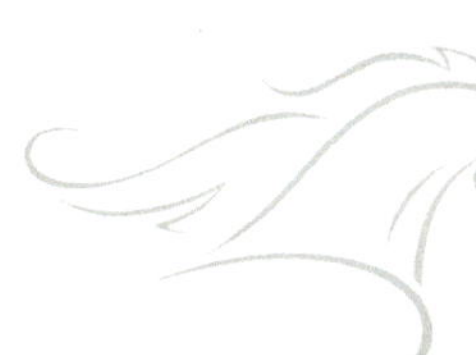

About the Author

BRADFORD G. WHELER is the former CEO, President and Co-owner of Allan Electric Company. He sold the company to a New York Stock Exchange listed company back when the stock market was hot. After staying on as President during the transition period, Brad retired.

Brad's lifelong love of history, art, books and the inherent humor in man's nature lead to the founding of BookCollaborative.com and the publishing of this book as well as "SNAPPY SAYINGS; wit & wisdom from the world's greatest minds" and "DOG SAYINGS; wit & wisdom from man's best friend."

Brad's various community involvements include being Chairman of the Board of Trustees of Cazenovia College, Former Chairman and a current member of the Board of Directors and Alumni Association and President of the Sigma Phi Society at Cornell University in Ithaca, NY. He is also a former member of the Board of Directors of the Greater Cazenovia Area Chamber of Commerce and several other boards.

Brad played polo on Cornell University's men's polo team for four years and was a member of the Cazenovia Polo Club.

Brad holds a BS and ME in Civil and Environmental Engineering from Cornell University in Ithaca, NY as well as an MBA degree from Fordham University in New York, NY.

Additionally, he is a Licensed Professional Engineer in New York and several other states. He is also a graduate of the Manlius Pebble Hill School. Brad, his wife Julie and their golden retriever Quincy live in Cazenovia, NY.

www.ingramcontent.com/pod-product-compliance
Lightning Source LLC
LaVergne TN
LVHW052252100826
845147LV00001B/24

* 9 7 8 0 9 8 2 2 5 3 8 3 0 *